inter\text

Language and Gender

The INTERTEXT series has been specifically designed to meet the needs of contemporary English Language Studies. *Working with Texts: A core introduction to language analysis* (3rd edition, 2007) is the foundation text, which is complemented by a range of 'satellite' titles. These provide students with hands-on practical experience of textual analysis through special topics, and can be used individually or in conjunction with *Working with Texts*.

Aimed at A-Level and beginning undergraduate students, *Language and Gender*:

- explores the relationship between language and our ideas about men and women
- challenges commonly held assumptions about language and gender
- investigates the process of stereotyping and the role of the individual in this process
- includes a comprehensive glossary of terms.

The book has been revised and updated to include:

- an additional chapter on gender, discourse and identities
- an integrated focus on gender, sexualisation and sexuality
- a more international and varied range of text types
- new data sources, such as social networking sites.

Angela Goddard is Professor of English Language at York St John University, UK, and Chair of Examiners for English Language A-Level at a national examination board.

Lindsey J. Meân is Assistant Professor in the Department of Communication Studies at Arizona State University, USA.

The Intertext series

The Routledge INTERTEXT series will develop readers' understanding of how texts work. It does this by showing some of the designs and patterns in the language from which they are made, by placing texts within the contexts in which they occur, and by exploring relationships between them.

The series consists of a foundation text, *Working with Texts: A core introduction to language analysis*, which looks at language aspects essential for the analysis of texts, and a range of satellite texts. These apply aspects of language to a particular topic area in more detail. They complement the core text and can also be used alone, providing the user has the foundation skills furnished by the core text.

Benefits of using this series:

- **Unique** – written by a team of respected teachers and practitioners whose ideas and activities have also been trialled independently.

- **Multi-disciplinary** – provides a foundation for the analysis of texts, supporting students who want to achieve a detailed focus on language.

- **Accessible** – no previous knowledge of language analysis is assumed, just an interest in language use.

- **Comprehensive** – wide coverage of different genres: literary texts, notes, signs, advertisements, leaflets, speeches, conversation.

- **Student-friendly** – contains suggestions for further reading; activities relating to texts studied; commentaries after activities; key terms highlighted and an index of terms.

The series editors:

Adrian Beard lectures in English Language and Linguistics at York St John University and is a Chief Examiner for AS- and A-Level English Literature. He has written extensively on the subjects of literature and language, his publications including *Texts and Contexts* (Routledge) and *The Language of Sport*, *The Language of Politics* and *Language Change* in this series.

Dr Angela Goddard is Head of Subject for Languages and Linguistics at York St John University. Her publications include *The Language of Advertising* in this series. Her current research interests are in aspects of identity and language use in computer-mediated communication. She is Chair of Examiners for English Language A-Level at a major national exam board.

Core textbook:

Working with Texts: A core introduction to language analysis (3rd edn; 2008) Ronald Carter, Angela Goddard, Danuta Reah, Keith Sanger, Nikki Swift

Satellite titles:

The Language of Advertising: Written texts
(2nd edn, 2002)
Angela Goddard

Language Change
Adrian Beard

The Language of Children
Julia Gillen

The Language of Comics
Mario Saraceni

The Language of Conversation
Francesca Pridham

The Language of Drama
Keith Sanger

The Language of Fiction
Keith Sanger

The Language of Humour
Alison Ross

The Language of ICT: Information and communication technology
Tim Shortis

The Language of Magazines
Linda McLoughlin

The Language of Newspapers
(2nd edn, 2002)
Danuta Reah

The Language of Poetry
John McRae

The Language of Politics
Adrian Beard

Language and Region
Joan C. Beal

The Language of Science
Carol Reeves

The Language of Speech and Writing
Sandra Cornbleet and Ronald Carter

The Language of Sport
Adrian Beard

The Language of Television
Jill Marshall and Angela Werndly

The Language of War
Steve Thorne

The Language of Websites
Mark Boardman

The Language of Work
Almut Koester

Language and Gender

◎ Angela Goddard
◎ Lindsey J. Meân

Routledge
Taylor & Francis Group

LONDON AND NEW YORK

First published 2000
This edition published 2009
by Routledge
2 Park Square, Milton Park, Abingdon, Oxon OX14 4RN

Simultaneously published in the USA and Canada
by Routledge
270 Madison Ave, New York, NY10016

Routledge is an imprint of the Taylor & Francis Group, an informa business

Typeset in Stone Sans and Stone Serif by
Florence Production Ltd, Stoodleigh, Devon
Printed and bound in Great Britain by
TJ International Ltd, Padstow, Cornwall

British Library Cataloguing in Publication Data
A catalogue record for this book is available from the British Library

Library of Congress Cataloging in Publication Data
Goddard, Angela, 1954–
  Language and gender / Angela Goddard and Lindsey Meân. – 2nd ed.
      p. cm. – (Intertext)
   Includes bibliographical references and index.
   1. Language and languages – Sex differences.   I. Patterson, Lindsey Meân,
   1964–   II. Title.
   P120.S48G63 2008
   306.44 – dc22   2008029015

ISBN10: 0–415–46663–6 (pbk)
ISBN13: 978–0–415–46663–9 (pbk)

contents

acknowledgements

The following texts and illustrations have been reprinted courtesy of their copyright holders:

O2 advert used by permission of O2 UK Limited.

Stonemarket catalogue 'cock and hen stone' image used by permission of Stonemarket Ltd, Warwickshire.

Catologue images used by permission of CompanyKids catalogue.

Lost Consonants No. 33 reproduced by permission of Graham Rawle.

Jak cartoon used by permission of the *Evening Standard/Solo* Syndication.

Images of clocks used by permission of KooKoo Bear Kids, Inc.

'The big C: Joan Smith asks why all the fuss over one little four-letter word' by Joan Smith. First published in *The Guardian*, G2, p. 5, 3 March 1998. Copyright © 1998 Joan Smith.

Extract from *Seduction* by Charlotte Lamb by permission of Harlequin Books S.A. First published by Mills and Boon® in Great Britain in 1980. Copyright © 1980 Charlotte Lamb.

'Men Talk' from *Dreaming Frankenstein* (1986) by Liz Lochhead is reprinted by permission of Polygon.

'The Mythical Chat Gap' by Ellen Goodman. First published in the *International Herald Tribune*, 20 July 2007.

Every effort has been made to trace and contact copyright holders. The publishers would be pleased to hear from any copyright holders not acknowledged here so that this acknowledgements page may be amended at the earliest opportunity.

Where appropriate, the presentation of previously published material may have been adapted to fit the requirements of this book.

The authors would like to thank all the people and organisations who gave their permission for the materials used in this book. Thank you also to Adrian Beard for being such a helpful, speedy and supportive editor, and to Ruth Faulkner, Ali Boyd and Rochelle Groves for finding some of the materials we used. Special love and thanks to Quinn.

introduction

This is a small book about a big area. The aim of this Introduction is to explain the rationale for the selection of material, and to clarify the meaning of certain important terms.

Sex and gender

First, the title *Language and Gender* refers to the relationship between language and our ideas about men and women. 'Gender' as a term differs from 'sex' in being about socially expected characteristics rather than biology. So, for instance, while possessing different genitalia is about biological factors, seeing this as leading to certain forms of behaviour is about gender.

One example of this process is the traditional idea in medicine and early psychology that people with wombs were more likely to be emotionally unstable. We can see this connection in the origin of the terms 'hysteria' and 'hysterical', which come from the Greek *husterikos*, meaning 'of the womb'. Hysterical behaviour has traditionally been associated with women, and their biology has been given as the 'cause'. In this case, as in many others, biology has been used to justify our social judgements, but this version of biology is itself socially constructed.

You may tell yourself that this is all distant history, and that, because there is no obvious biological reference in the term 'hysterical', there is no issue to discuss here. But would you, even now, describe a man as being 'hysterical'? If not, is that because men don't behave in that way, or is it because this same behaviour in men would be called something else, perhaps something more positive?

Man/woman, male/female, masculine/feminine

While the terms 'man' and 'woman' can refer to definitions based on biological differences, the terms 'masculine' and 'feminine' are always about expected gender characteristics – what men and women are supposed to be like. The 'ine' ending itself means 'like', as in 'bovine' (like a cow), 'vulpine' (like a wolf), 'Geraldine' (like a Gerald). (No, that last example wasn't a mistake.)

While 'man' and 'woman' are nouns and therefore suggest 'people', 'masculine' and 'feminine' are adjectives and suggest qualities or attributes. So we could talk about 'masculine women' and 'feminine men' and be thinking about people who depart from the norm of what we consider appropriate for each sex. There is a third pair of terms – 'male' and 'female' – that can and often do shift between positions, according to the writer's intentions. If people talk about 'males' and 'females', they could be using the terms as nouns, as alternatives to 'men' and 'women'; but these terms can also function as adjectives, like 'masculine' and 'feminine'. So a writer might be talking of 'male behaviour' and really mean 'masculine behaviour'.

If you are going to get to grips with the ideas above, you need to do some practical investigating. As is true of all the satellite texts in the INTERTEXT series, this book aims to give you some starting points for research of your own. But the topic of language and gender is a bit different from others in this series, in that there is already much published material on it, aimed at different age groups and operating at different levels. In particular, many textbooks aimed at secondary age students cover the idea of sexism in language and images, especially in the mass media. It is therefore likely that you will have 'done' this topic, perhaps several times, over the course of your school/college career. So why do it all over again in this book?

It isn't the case that, just because you've 'done' gender as a topic, there's nothing else to say. For a start, you need to ask *how* you studied this topic: what were the assumptions behind the thinking you were given, and that you yourself did? Also, research in this area has changed considerably over the years: how do you know that you're not stuck in the 1970s?

The following comments are taken from student essays, and they show some commonly expressed ideas on language and gender:

'The English language is sexist.'

'Sex stereotyping is all the fault of the media and of society.'

'Women use powerless language and that makes them inferior.'

In this book we want to challenge ideas such as these in the following ways:

- People often put the blame for stereotyping elsewhere – for example, it's in the language itself, it's the fault of the media, it's to do with 'society'. They tend not to include themselves in their account. Our aim is to show how we all 'do' gender in our everyday thinking.

- Looking at everyday thinking means looking at psychological processes and at social organisation. It's not enough just to look at language without considering how it relates to wider issues about how we think and understand, and how we view our own and others' social groups. So, for example, saying that a particular term is 'stereotyped' doesn't get us very far without some exploration of what the process of stereotyping might be about.

- There are many books on the subject of the linguistic usages of men and women, particularly on the differences between them. But the very fact that there is a lot of research causes a problem: how can you assess where any one article or textbook stands in the history of research in this area? For example, current ideas about 'powerless language' are certainly not those described above. So, rather than offering a catalogue of 'differences' – which you can easily get from elsewhere if you want them – we are offering ways for you to think about any account of 'difference' that you may read.

Because of the nature of what we are trying to do, you may well find that this book varies in how it works interactively: there are many activities, but there are also some sections that ask you to read blocks of text and think. So be prepared for some variation.

Projections

Aim of this unit

The aim of this unit is to get you thinking about the relationship between the language we use and the world around us. Consideration of this is important when looking at language and gender, because we need to establish how far our ideas about the sexes are the result of seeing what we want to see – or, rather, seeing what we *have* to see because of the language that is available to us.

The Sapir-Whorf hypothesis

The issue of whether language is simply a direct reflection of the world around us has been debated for many centuries. For example, the Ancient Greek philosopher, Socrates, asked questions about whether there was any intrinsic connection between an object and its name. In more recent times, the linguist, Edward Sapir, and the psychologist, Benjamin Lee Whorf, found themselves asking questions in the same broad area of language and thought as a result of their anthropological work with speakers of different languages, particularly North American Indian languages. They concluded that we are not simply passive recorders of what we find around us in language; rather, we impose our ideas on our environment as a result of the language we have.

1

This is how they put this concept, which has come to be termed 'The Sapir-Whorf hypothesis':

> We dissect nature along lines laid down by our native languages. The categories and types that we isolate from the world of phenomena we do not find there because they stare every observer in the face; on the contrary, the world is presented in a kaleidoscopic flux of impressions which has to be organized by our minds – and this means largely by the linguistic systems in our minds.
>
> (Whorf, 1956, p. 213)

In other words, when we acquire language, we acquire ways of thinking – conceptual systems or grids – which we don't notice consciously because they just feel natural to us. It's a bit like viewing the world through a particular pair of spectacles that we've become used to wearing. And these spectacles are our culture. Some speakers – bilingual language users, for example – have more than one pair of spectacles. And here, speakers readily attest to the fact that they think differently when they use their different languages. Professional interpreters spend their working lives trying to match a set of concepts from one language with the words of another. And, sometimes, there are gaps where an idea in one language is simply not encoded in another. For example, in Russian, there are no words to label 'hand' or 'foot' as separate from the arm or leg. Examples such as these give us evidence of the existence of the Sapir-Whorf 'linguistic systems' mentioned above.

Further practical examples of different languages encoding 'reality' differently are easy to find. One of the most commonly quoted areas is colour terms. English, for example, has 11 basic words for colours – white, black, red, green, yellow, blue, brown, purple, pink, orange and grey. (This list does not include terms for colours that are incorporated in other colours – for example, beige is a form of brown, sage is a form of green, and so on.) In contrast, speakers of some New Guinea Highland languages have only two terms: 'dark' and 'light'. It's clear that, in labelling colours, speakers of different languages chop up the spectrum in different ways – as in Text 1:1, where some English and Welsh terms are mapped against each other. What's harder to determine is whether this means the speakers of different languages actually see differently when they look at the same colour.

Text 1:1 Colour terms map

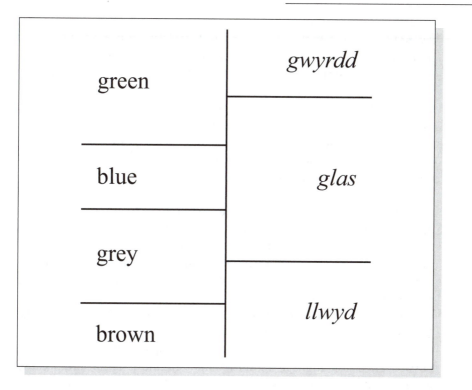

Another aspect of describing colour that appears to vary on a language basis is metaphorical reference. For example, where English speakers talk of 'blue jokes', in Spanish these are 'green' (but in Mexican Spanish, 'red' (Jones, 1999)); while 'green' for English speakers has at least two sets of connotations: ecologically minded, and unpractised (with the suggestion of naivety). English has many negative connotations for the term 'black', which have been seen as the cultural legacy of a white-dominated society. Black is used for bereavement, in contrast to the white clothes people wear to funerals in India. In English, white often stands for purity, while red connotes danger (or anger, as in 'seeing red') and yellow connotes cowardice. The list is long, but that doesn't mean there's any logic in any of the relationships between the colour terms and the ideas that they call up for any group of speakers. These meanings are **arbitrary**: if we have associations for a particular colour term, it's more likely to be because we put them there than because they occurred somehow 'naturally'. If they occurred naturally, then everyone would have the same system.

The way speakers establish categories in language can be shown to relate to what they need language for – in other words, what the preoccupations are in their particular community. Frequently discussed examples of this are that Inuit people have different words for snow, nomadic Arabic groups many words for different types of camel, and Australian aboriginal languages many words for different types of hole in the sand. Different lifestyles mean that some groups need to pay more attention than others to particular aspects of the environment, leading to more or less fine **discriminations** within language categories. These discriminations are important for the members of the community in question: a mistake about the weight that a patch of snow can bear, about the value of a camel, or about the type of creature that may inhabit a hole in the sand, all have real-life consequences. Snow, camels and sand-holes all have 'reality', but the fine distinctions between the various different types are unlikely to be noticed by outsiders, for whom variations are not significant, or **salient**. If variations are noticed, they will be seen as minor variations that can easily be accommodated by the single terms they already have: to people from a temperate climate, snow is just snow, whatever its condition.

But languages don't only differ in the names they have for objects. They also differ in how they organise abstract ideas, such as ways of talking about relationships, or the qualities that people have. And here the possible effects of language upon thought seem more significant, because we are talking about our social values, how we treat each other and organise ourselves within society. However, abstract ideas are more elusive to grasp than the names of objects, and their effects are more difficult to plot.

A common way of understanding how language is organised and influences thought is through the concept of **discourses**. Language is considered to be structured into a number of discourses that 'show up' in what people say, write and do. This means that discourses influence which words and concepts are widely used and how they get understood.

As a brief initial exploration of the Sapir-Whorf hypothesis, consider the following and answer the questions below.

Swedish speakers have a term – *sambo* (bo = 'live', pronounced 'boo') – for a person they are living with but not married to. They also have the further terms below for people they are involved with:

sarbo	to refer to a partner who does not live with the speaker;
narbo	to refer to a partner who lives close to the speaker – e.g. a few streets away;
delsbo	to refer to a partner who has a house of their own, but with whom the speaker lives for part of the time (*dels* = 'partly').

None of these terms is marked for the sex of the person who is being referred to (Hudson, 1999).

In English, we can refer to a person with whom we are having a love relationship in at least the following ways:

my lover;
my partner;
my girlfriend/my boyfriend;
my friend;
my significant other.

* Can you add any further terms you use to the English list?
* If you speak another language, what are the choices in that language?
* Are you happy with the terms you can choose from, or do you think there are gaps? If there are gaps, what is it that you cannot express satisfactorily?
* To what extent do the English terms force you to specify the sex of the person you are involved with?
* Do you think that different groups in society might use the terms on the list in different ways? For example, how might a speaker's age or sexual orientation affect their choices and intended meanings?
* What ideas are encoded by the Swedish terms? Would you find the Swedish categories useful? What might their existence within the Swedish system suggest about Swedish culture?

Commentary

The responses you gathered to the questions above are likely to have varied according to a number of factors. The notes here are just an indication of some of the possible variables. One piece of recent research (Harvey, 1997), which surveyed usage among straight and gay male users of English, found that age was significant for straight men in that the term 'girlfriend' suggested youth. Beyond that, the term 'partner' was seen by straight men as suggesting permanence and seriousness of relationship, while 'lover' suggested something less serious. However, gay men had different readings for some of the terms. For example, gay men saw the term 'boyfriend' as giving a more long-term, serious message about the relationship (regardless of the age factor) than 'lover'. Many of the gay interviewees commented that the term they chose would very much depend on who they were talking to and what environment they were in.

This activity was designed to get you thinking about the available options in any one language system. Aside from the way in which different languages present different options, however, it is important to realise that there are different groups within the same language system who might be served more or less well by the options available. Analysis of different usage and meanings can reveal the different discourses underlying the system of meaning being used. For example, there is a common understanding in some parts of the US that the term 'partner' would *only* be used in a same-sex relationship, which contrasts with its usage elsewhere as a term that explicitly avoids denoting gender.

A broad point to make about the language choices presented here is that choices are clearly subject to change. For example, the term 'partner' is a relatively new phenomenon. This means that the Sapir-Whorf hypothesis cannot be true in any extreme way, otherwise language change of this kind would never be possible. New social practices and configurations – in this case, people deciding to live together rather than get married – cause new language to emerge. But the fact that people want their experiences to be named at all should tell us something about the role of language, which is clearly to validate and legitimise a person's behaviour and interpretations. The feeling that a word lends a sense of reality to an idea proves how powerful language is in our reading of the world.

Anthropomorphism

Anthropomorphism means 'giving something a human shape' and describes another kind of projection that we often see in language. Exploration of this area will provide some more exemplification of the relationship between language and thought.

Perhaps human beings are essentially very lonely and insecure creatures: it seems that we need constantly to project the idea of humanness on to the inanimate world. We make cartoons for children in which objects such as brooms and spoons talk and sing; one of our most successful credit card adverts in the 1980s featured a nervous Cockney-speaking pound sign called Money and his confident flexible friend, Access; we give our cars affectionate names and even call death-making bombs and hurricanes after human beings. Perhaps we hope that, if we can humanise the inanimate world, it will seem friendlier and therefore less terrifying. The persuasive potential of this anthropomorphism is not lost on advertisers (see the advert in Text 1:2).

Text 1:2 House

As well as giving animacy to inanimate objects, we also 'humanise' the animal kingdom, often giving characteristics to animals that are completely unrelated to their behaviour in their natural habitat. For example, no one who has ever observed wild bears would think of them as the cuddly, soft items that populate the current 'Teddy Bear' shops. Of course, there is no harm in humanising animals for the purposes of entertainment. But the ways in which we do this can tell us something about ourselves and how we perpetuate certain ideas or discourses.

Activity

- What characteristics do we ascribe to the animals in the following list?

- To what extent are these characteristics projections by humans on to the animals?

- Can you think of any other animals that we describe in particular ways?

snake	fox	lamb
slug	wolf	owl
shark	pig	rat
cat	dog	worm

- What do we mean when we say the following about humans?

He/she is . . .

a snake	a rat
a fox	a cat
a lamb	a pussycat
a slug	a tiger
a wolf	a dog
a shark	a worm
a pig	a mouse

- Do the animal names above vary according to the sex of the person being referred to? For example, are some used more often to describe one sex than the other? Are some used for both sexes, but mean something different when used about one sex or the other?

Many American sports teams, and a few British, use animal names. There is no reason that we know of why animal names are so widely adopted in

American sport, or why there are fewer in British sport. But the selection of a team name is a significant issue. So why do you think the American Football and (Ice) Hockey teams listed below chose these particular animals? What are the characteristics they were intending to connote?

Baltimore Bengals	St Louis Rams	Florida Panthers
Phoenix Coyotes	San Jose Sharks	Anaheim Ducks
Nashville Predators	Pittsburgh Penguins	Denver Broncos
Indianapolis Colts	Jacksonville Jaguars	Miami Dolphins
Atlanta Falcons	Carolina Panthers	Chicago Bears
Detroit Lions	Philadelphia Eagles	Seattle Seahawks

Commentary

You may have noted some prevalent patterns of the animals' characteristics that overlap with characteristics valued in sport, such as athleticism, strength and ferociousness. Killer instinct and hunting prowess are also characteristics associated with many of the animals, invoking ideas about competitiveness and 'survival of the fittest', which are also prevalent concepts in sport discourses. So it is easy to understand why the athletic panther and ferocious shark were selected. But some of these animals have much less obviously desirable characteristics for a sport team. For example, why do you think Pittsburgh selected a penguin? Of course it is easy to look for the familiar sound repetition, but sometimes greater specific knowledge or local information reveal a different understanding about the relationships between things. In this case, the nickname of the team's home venue, the 'Igloo', apparently accounts for the choice 'Penguins'.

'God bless her, and all who sail in her'

So far, we have looked at the way we project human qualities on to both inanimate objects and animals. But, as the previous activity suggested, we also project gender. The title above is part of a well-known ritual whereby a ship is launched and blessed. But why is it not: 'God bless it, and all who sail in it'? Or even: 'God bless him, and all who sail in him'?

Some commentators (for example, Spender, 1980) have suggested that cars, as well as boats, are seen as female because they are objects of status that have traditionally been under the control of men. Certainly, the physical attractiveness of such objects is often at the forefront of descriptions, in the same way that women are often described in terms of their looks. For example, here is an extract from a news report on the decommissioning of the Royal Yacht *Britannia*:

> a ship which has given good faithful service for 44 years, and which is still as elegant now as when she was commissioned.
>
> (Radio 4 *News*, 10 December 1997)

If Spender is right about why some objects are personified as female, it doesn't follow that it's only men who use language in this way, nor does it mean that every usage of this kind is a conscious one. Spender is talking about a male perspective, or way of viewing the world, that is encoded in the language we all use as a common resource. And it is precisely because we use language without analysing each and every item that a way of thinking can exist without really being noticed. It is only when our flow of language is disrupted that we become conscious of the thinking that is embedded in language – and then we can ask whose thinking it really is. Here is an example of that process in action. The news journalist, Sue McGregor, in covering a world energy conference, is talking to another journalist about Britain's past record on industrial pollution:

> but Britain's been a good boy, hasn't she ... or he? (*nervous laughter*).
>
> (Radio 4 *Today Programme*, 9 December 1997)

Sue McGregor finds it difficult to continue her presentation of Britain as a 'good boy' because as soon as a **pronoun reference** is needed, 'she' emerges automatically, causing the journalist some confusion and embarrassment. It appears that, as far as pronouns are concerned, our ideas about the gender of not just mechanical objects, but also countries, are deeply embedded in our thinking. Countries are so often depicted as female, as in the headline in Text 1:3, that, if the headline had read:

> AMERICA REVEALS HIS POLICY ON GLOBAL WARMING: TOO LITTLE, TOO LATE

then it would seem as though America was revealing the policy of a male individual (perhaps the President?). In other words, the 'his' would not appear connected to 'America' at all.

Text 1:3 *Independent* **headline**

THE INDEPENDENT

Thursday 23 October 1997   45p No. 3,435 ****

America reveals her policy on global warming: too little, too late

Countries do not always appear as 'she', however. For example, during the period of Fascist rule in Germany leading up to the Second World War, Germany was often referred to in Fascist literature as the 'Fatherland'. But it's interesting to note the link between the idea of Germany as male and the qualities that were being stressed – not Germany's ability to feed and nurture its people, but the military might of the country, its readiness for adversity. Pronoun usage therefore appears to be part of a larger picture in which we use notions of male and female to stand for different sets of qualities. The pages that follow will explore this is more detail, as will the next unit.

Mother Nature, Father Time

The use of 'she' to refer to a country often appears to go along with the idea of a matriarchal figure originating and sustaining its people (as in 'mother country' and 'mother tongue'). This idea is also encoded in the idea of 'Mother Nature', a nurturing, protecting force. In a popular children's cartoon, 'SuperTed', the teddy bear figure, initially a factory reject, is claimed by Mother Nature and given superpowers to fight wrongdoing. Mother Nature, with her friendly wand, here resembles a fairy godmother, a very different figure from that traditionally associated with 'Father Time', who is often pictured as stern, authoritarian and inhumane:

Time hath, my lord, a wallet at his back,
Wherein he puts alms for oblivion,

A great-sized monster of ingratitudes:
Those scraps are good deeds past; which are devoured
As fast as they are made, forgot as soon
As done.

> (Shakespeare, *Troilus and Cressida*, Act III, iii: 145–50)

Sometimes, gender projections on to the inanimate world appear to encode qualities that are polar opposites. They occur in a wide range of different domains, from the kind of visual **metonymy** represented by the 'cock' and 'hen' stones (Text 1:4), which represent the idea of high and low respectively, to the aural differences represented by the 'male' and 'female' endings of poetry lines. The male ending (also called a 'strong' ending) represents a stressed syllable at the end of the line, while a female ending (also called a 'weak' ending) has an unstressed syllable. This is exemplified below, where the first and third lines have feminine endings, and the rest, masculine endings:

'Tis Spring, come out to ramble (F)
The hilly brakes around, (M)
For under thorn and bramble (F)
About the hollow ground (M)
The primroses are found. (M)

> (A.E. Housman, 'The Lent Lily', in Horwood, 1971)

Text 1:4 Garden catalogue

COCK & HEN STONE EDGING

The appearance of random stones laid on edge has been attained within one easy to lay unit. The natural rustic look has been re-created by following the traditional laying method of raising and lowering stones on edge in 'cock & hen' fashion. Ideal as a border for driveways, pathways or flowerbeds and can be used as a topping stone for Yorkstone and Cotstone Walling.

Size 21" x 7" x 6"

LANDSCAPE NOTE
Decorative Edging units may be butted together and simply laid onto a good level surface, or shallow earth trough, or for a permanent fix, bed on a 'stiff' mix concrete foundation.

Dogtooth Edging is a Registered Design

The habit of thinking about the genders as opposites appears firmly embedded in our ways of understanding and our representational practices. A classic example is 'male' and 'female' fittings for electrical and plumbing connections: there are many other ways that the plumbing connections shown in Text 1:5 could have been labelled.

Text 1:5 Plumbing connections

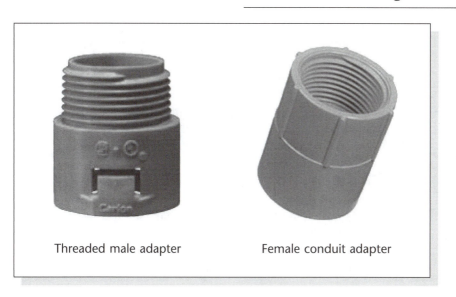

Threaded male adapter   Female conduit adapter

The sex life of seals

Natural history programmes are useful sources of evidence for investigating anthropomorphism and, within this, projections of gender. Such programmes are particularly important because they are often cited as proof that human beings are, or should be, 'naturally' disposed to behave in a certain way. The argument goes: look, the animals, our relatives, do it this way, so it must be only natural for us to do so. But the question is, do the human observers record objectively what they see, or do they project on to the animal world aspects of human behaviour, with all our attached ideas of relationships between male and female human beings?

Academics who have researched the way wildlife programmes are presented (e.g. Coward, 1984; Crowther and Leith, 1995) claim that such

13

programmes involve humans projecting on to the animal world aspects of human behaviour, which they then 'find' there and claim as evidence for a natural order. A further claim is that such presentations consist overwhelmingly of male scientists talking to each other and presenting their stories about animals from the perspective of the male animals they are observing.

Activity

Text 1:6 is an extract from the Radio 4 *Natural History Programme*, 7 December 1997. The presenter (A) travels to a remote Scottish island called North Rona to meet a researcher (B) who is studying grey seals. Both A and B are male.

- To what extent are the human speakers anthropomorphising the animals they are talking about? Can you find examples of language that might be more appropriate to describe human relationships than those of animals?
- How are the male and female animals presented in the programme?
- Is the account presented from the point of view of male, or female, animals? How might the account have differed if it had taken the point of view of another group?

Note that there is no commentary on this activity.

Text 1:6 Natural history dialogue

> A: ... But anyway, its grey seals that we 're here to see and, er, I'm gonna drop down on the cliff now and meet [name of researcher] of [name of university], a researcher there, and he works specifically on the male grey seal. We're sitting in a sea of seals and, er, all looking like huge great maggots on this great big glassy slope and in fact two are fighting right in front of us.
>
> B: Oh, that's not actually a fight, that's sex really, believe it or not. That's the dominant male for this, er, group of females that we're, er, sitting above here and, er, he's basically showing his passions for her, basically. The average duration of copulation is about 20 minutes but they can actually last up to well over an hour. I think

the longest one I've observed is 65 minutes. I think that's basically as long as the male needs to mate with a female to actually inseminate her.

A: The odd cry, the odd huge snort with masses of mucus flying out of their nostrils, about sort of two yards. Well, listen to him, he, he growls rather like a bear. Bears might be quite a good way to describe them because they're actually very hairy, aren't they?

B: They are. In many ways their behavioural postures, even though they've got very short flippers, are very bear-like or at least dog-like anyway.

A: Oh he charged him – a great big growl, a great snap at the back of his hind flippers.

B: Yeah, they don't like being bitten round the hind flippers, that's where they're very vulnerable.

A: And you can hear him sort of flopping along like a great big sort of caterpillar. Well, just to paint a picture for everybody 'cos it really is amazing, what we're looking at. There must be three or four hundred animals, goodness knows how many in front of us and of the animals that we can see, we can see lots are obviously pups, those gorgeous white velvety animals with huge great big dishy eyes, and um, lots of mottled coloured animals which are much bigger and, they're the females, and considerably fewer but much larger animals, these great big sort of warriors, the bulls.

B: That's it, the sex ratio of adult females to adult males on the breeding colony is about one male to seven females and the males will stay here for up to eight or nine weeks at a time without feeding but relying on their blubber reserves and trying to mate with as many females as possible.

A: And even as a lay person looking at these animals I can see that there's a male surrounded by several females and that pattern is repeated across the whole of this hillside right down to the sea.

B: It is effectively a polygamous system, each of the successful males will probably mate with 10 to 12 females during the breeding season. There's a lot of males that don't manage to get any copulations at all, but it's very different strategies that the males employ such as these resident males we see before us sitting amongst their groups of females, they're very socially dominant – they will chase off other males and engage in aggressive interactions.

A: We've seen lots of fights, haven't we? I mean, these fights are posturing. I mean they draw blood, but they are vicious, aren't they?

B: The really vicious fights tend to be between neighbouring resident males because they're very equally matched and when they eventually do come to blows they are fairly severe fights.

A: They're like real warriors if they, if they win over that . . . I mean, they posture right up, don't they; 'I'm the winner of this one!'

B: They quite often roll on their back and wave their foreflippers in the air, as well as a sort of a victory gesture.

A: And this male mating right in front of us now, he's a warrior, he's a successful male.

B: He's been here right from the start of the season and he's doing very well already – he's had six copulations that I've observed anyway. But you'll notice occasionally other males – there is one over here which is, you may have more difficulty in distinguishing him from a female.

A: Yes, he looks very like a female. I mean he's actually really low down on the grass, he's kind of rather roman-nosed, sort of bent over contours of the tussock grass.

B: Indeed, he's, er, much smaller and sleeker and as you notice he's not got much scarring on him. Ah this male strategy is very different – he'll basically sneak around almost pretending to be a female and er . . .

A: Warrior in a girl's blouse.

B: Yeah, and he'll keep out of the way of trouble and if one of the resident males comes towards him to threaten him, he'll just run away, he'll bolt and hide somewhere and then when the resident male disappears again to go and check out some female he'll sneak back in again and just lie down and wait and when you watch one of these more peripheral males trying to mate with a female there's often far more aggression from the female, they'll really object to that mating. In some cases it almost amounts to a rape, the male forces a copulation on the female.

A: Why does he do that? I mean, he doesn't have to engage in fights. I can see the advantage there but he picks up a huge resistance from the females and these females are no mean match, I mean, they are big and they've got lots of teeth, they could inflict a lot of damage I would have thought.

B: That's true, but there's also a cost to being a resident male. As I said, these resident males will stay for the whole breeding season, they lose about two kilograms of weight a day, relying on their blubber reserves. They're not feeding and towards the end of the season you see these resident males and they're basically just a bag of bones, basically, and they're scarred and bloodied from the encounters with their neighbouring resident males.

A: I see, so these peripheral males are cheats, really.

B: They run around a lot, they're very active and mobile but they avoid the serious fights from the males, they get more aggression from the females, certainly.

A: And are they always cheaters, or do they turn into warriors?

B: Well, that's an interesting question, we've got one friend just up the slope here and he's been here since 1987, my first year out here, and he started out as one of these run-around males and he graduated slowly into a more resident male and this year he's holding himself a nice position amongst a good group of females and doing very well.

Summary

This unit has suggested that language is not a neutral reflection of the world around us, but that, by using language, we project on to the world our own sense of 'reality'. Starting with the idea that different languages encode objects and ideas differently, we then went on to look at two specific types of projection: the projection of humanness on to the inanimate world; and the projection of gender on to the inanimate and animal worlds. The next unit will explore further the idea of the different qualities that are seen as the appropriate domain of one sex or the other.

Extension activities

1   Research all the terms in the English language using 'black' and 'white': for example, 'a black look', a 'white lie'. To what extent do terms using black and white encode negative and positive meanings?

2   Make a list of all the colours that are used in English metaphorically: for example, 'I'm feeling blue' to mean 'I'm feeling depressed'. Then research the way one other language uses different colour terms metaphorically. If you are familiar with another language yourself, you could go on to consider some further areas of English and your other language where you feel there are differences in how ideas are expressed.

3   Research the use of relationship terms (lover, boyfriend, etc.). Pay attention to the idea that different groups may have different readings of the terms, and therefore different usage patterns for them.

4   (a)   What animals are used to construct fantasy figures within our popular cultural stories (for example, fairy stories, horror films, comic heroes/heroines)?

    (b)   What animal names are used to construct terms of abuse by each sex about the other?

    (c)   What animal names are used as address terms and reference items in lovers' messages to each other (for example, in Valentine's messages in newspapers)?

    From answering the questions above, what do you conclude about the way human beings categorise animals and use them within our own referencing system? What human feelings and attitudes are evident, both about the animals and about ourselves?

5   Watch or visit the websites of some popular television programmes for toddlers. Many of these programmes are inhabited by animals or inanimate objects that have been given 'human' characteristics. Which animals have been chosen for what sort of characters, and what characteristics are associated with them? Have they been given a gender? How do you know which gender they have been given? What physical, emotional or behavioural characteristics make them male or female?

6   Record and transcribe a natural history programme from the TV or radio, and consider some of the questions that were explored in this unit about anthropomorphism and projections of gender. In particular, you might ask:

(a)   What sex are the presenters and experts?

(b)   What aspects of animal behaviour are the focus of the programme? Why do you think these aspects have been selected?

(c)   What evidence is there that the animals are being described in anthropomorphic ways?

(d)   Is the account being presented from the point of view of male animals, female animals, or both?

Making up gender

Aims of this unit

The previous unit emphasised the way we project animacy and gender on to the world around us. In this unit, we will be looking at the qualities and characteristics we associate with men and women. We will do this by looking at the language we use to describe the sexes, and asking how far this language is a reflection of our learned beliefs.

This unit is called 'making up gender' for at least two reasons: one is to question whether the way we view the sexes is in any sense 'natural'; another is to suggest that we 'make up' gender as we go along. This means that, far from being a fixed and unalterable dimension that is imposed on us from on high, gender is something that we do every day as part of our social behaviour. But this doesn't mean that gender is something we simply choose or don't choose to do. While ideas about gender changing over time and across cultures show us that gender isn't a fixed concept, current ideas about gender still influence the ways in which we 'do' gender – whether we are conforming to or challenging the dominant gender discourses.

Bodies of description

In school, we are taught that adjectives describe items and nouns name or label them. As usual, such apparent simplicities disguise quite a lot of complexity. For a start, adjectives operate at a number of different levels. For example, the dictionary definition of a word – its **denotation** – is hardly ever the end of the story. A very potent aspect of meaning is the level of **connotation** a word can call up – all the associated ideas we connect with a term. Connotation is a fluid aspect of meaning, as it will depend not only on the experiences that individuals and groups bring to interactions, but also on who is using the terms and how they are being deployed.

As an illustration of the potential differences between denotation and connotation, consider the word 'bald'. The dictionary definition of this term is 'having the scalp wholly or partly hairless', but the connotations of this label can be very negative and go beyond a purely physical description.

As well as one adjective having connotations that are very different from its denotative meaning, there are also pairs of adjectives that have the same denotation but very different connotations. For example, 'someone without children' could be the denotation of both the terms 'childless' and 'childfree', but these terms have nothing in common at the connotative level of meaning.

Just as adjectives can operate at different levels of description, so can nouns. Nouns are traditionally not thought of as descriptors; they are seen as labelling words, with the implication that things exist prior to their needing a name. At the simplest level, it is true that one of the functions of language is to name and itemise the world around us: tables, chairs and computers need to be called something. But, when you get away from concrete objects, naming isn't quite so cut and dried. For example, here are two common nouns that refer to people:

bachelor   spinster

At the level of denotation, these terms mean 'unmarried adult male' and 'unmarried adult female', respectively. However, the connotations of these two nouns go much further: while a bachelor is traditionally seen as a man who has *chosen* not to marry and who is 'playing the field', a spinster is seen as a woman who has *failed* to find a husband and who has been 'left on the shelf'. Our everyday expressions, such as those in quotation marks in the previous sentence, also reveal a lot about our hidden thinking. Men are associated with sport; women, not just with shopping, but with being saleable commodities that are, in this case, past their sell-by date.

The point being made above is that even nouns, looking for all the world like simple, clear-cut labels, are categories that often mask a whole range of implicit descriptions that are very revealing of cultural values. Implicit meanings are very powerful precisely because they are unremarkable and therefore can become part of our automatic thinking.

Implicitness in itself is not necessarily a bad thing, however: as an aspect of language use, we employ it on a daily basis to make our communication more economic than it would otherwise be. For example, we can imply a great deal about people's characteristics, qualities, moods and physical states just by selecting a particular verb + adverb combination. If a friend tells you that they are *swotting frantically* for an exam, this might conjure up a picture of someone in a state of nervous exhaustion, feeling that they are running out of time, panicking, burning the midnight oil, drinking cups of black coffee to stay awake. Similarly, the choice of one particular verb over another to describe an action constructs a picture of the person being described. For example, even without the adverb 'frantically', if your friend said they were *revising* instead of swotting, or *reviewing* their work, your picture would be likely to be one of considerably more calm control.

Such language choices enable us to be economic because a lot can be left unsaid: the speaker or writer knows that the listener/reader can fill in the gaps as a result of the thinking that is shared by members of cultural groups who speak the same language.

Activity

Listed in the table overleaf are some verb + adverb combinations for the verbs 'to run' and 'to eat'. In the right-hand column are alternative verbs. What sort of physical characteristics, personality characteristics and emotional states are implied by the descriptions?

23

Category	Verb + adverb	Variant verb
to run	she ran merrily she ran jauntily she ran slowly she ran doggedly she ran jerkily she ran gracefully she ran crazily	she pelted she raced she legged it she sped she jogged she skipped she ambled she lumbered she gambolled
to eat	he ate sloppily he ate voraciously he ate greedily he ate thoughtfully he ate warily he ate daintily he ate noisily he ate carefully	he stuffed (himself) he pigged out he savoured he gorged he picked at his food he played with his food he slurped he nibbled he gobbled he dined he supped he chomped

Commentary

The descriptions above often suggest quite clear pictures of physical movement. For example, when you thought about the phrase 'she ran jerkily' you probably pictured a female figure throwing out her arms at odd angles, perhaps running at tangents rather than in a straight line. But, after establishing a physical picture, a sense of the runner's state of mind also suggests itself: why is she running jerkily? What has happened to her, and what is she feeling? Some of the other examples above take us more directly to a psychological state: 'she ran doggedly' perhaps says more about the runner's determination and perseverance than her physical behaviour; attitude rather than running style.

Notice that, in the second sentence of the paragraph above, it says 'you probably pictured a *female* figure . . .'. Another aspect of the way you made sense of the verbal language above was to picture the person who was performing the actions as either male or female. You were told to do this by the language of the examples: 'she' was doing all the running, 'he' was doing all the eating. You may have felt, though, that this unspecified male and female weren't always behaving as you might expect, as some terms tend to be used more about one sex than the other. For example, are 'he ate daintily' and 'he nibbled' typical phrases to describe a man? What about 'she legged it', to describe the actions of a woman, compared with 'she skipped'? Would it be a different kind of woman who would 'leg it', compared with one who would 'skip'? Would 'he skipped' be likely to occur in descriptions of an adult male? If so, what kind of man would be pictured?

All the questions raised above relate to the beliefs we have about the way men and women typically behave – their gender characteristics; those aspects we expect to be present as a result of being male or female. And our expectations are constantly validated by the operation of **collocation** in language use: the way in which words and phrases occur over and over again in certain predictable contexts – such as next to or near the words 'man' and 'woman', for example. The activity below explores the gender dimension of the company that words keep.

Activity

Read through the terms below and sort them into two lists, according to whether you think the terms are more commonly used with reference to men or to women. You could then include a third list, where you think the terms can be used of either sex, but where the meaning changes according to which sex is being referred to. Can you detect any patterns in the types of words used to refer to one sex or the other?

tactful	athletic	emotional	ambitious	slim
dominant	pretty	elegant	aggressive	neat
independent	nurturing	intellectual	bubbly	neurotic
impassive	graceful	strong	empathic	agile
competitive	chatty	controlled	muscular	well-built
beautiful	handsome	fragile	bright	bimbo
hunk	kind	capable	gentle	buxom
physique	figure	rugged	tearful	hysterical

Commentary

The terms you have been working with refer both to physical and to personality characteristics. You may have found that, in both respects, the terms that you associated with a male **referent** differed from those you more often see associated with a female referent.

In some cases, terms are exclusively used only about one sex or the other. For example, in describing men and women physically, men tend to have 'physiques', while women have 'figures'. The connotations of these two terms are very different: physique suggests physical strength and body size, while figure connotes aesthetic shapeliness and sexual attractiveness. Only men can be hunky and only women buxom, with the latter term being a very specific reference to breast size, while hunkiness is a much more general attribute. Sometimes, the same term could be used to describe both sexes, but the implications might differ: for example, 'well-built' could mean 'a well-developed physique' when applied to a man, but when applied to a woman could be a **euphemism** for buxom, or even fat. One recent study of collocations for the terms 'man' and 'woman' (Herriman, 1998) based on the Cobuild corpus (a collection of language texts of all kinds, totalling 50 million words) found that words for physical attractiveness (pretty, sexy, glamorous) collocated most frequently with 'woman', while terms to describe height, abilities and personality most frequently collocated with 'man'.

Some terms can be used to suggest either physical characteristics or personality traits. For example, strength can be a psychological ability as well as a physical one: someone can be 'as strong as an ox'; they can also have 'the strength to cope'. How you interpreted this word will have made a difference to your results, as, while men are often seen as stronger than women physically, their psychological strength might be more readily disputed (although the referent for the phrase 'a strong silent type' is usually male).

Terms describing personality traits, such as 'chatty' or 'aggressive', can often be seen to fall into certain predictable patterns when used to describe the sexes. Research has consistently shown that people will willingly and easily identify characteristics that are typically male or female, but that have little to do with the actual attributes of real individuals. Morgan (1986, p. 179) notes a number of qualities that are typically associated with males and females in Western society. Males are seen as logical, rational, aggressive, exploitative, strategic, independent and competitive. Females are thought to be intuitive, emotional, submissive, empathic, spontaneous, nurturing and co-operative. Morgan summarises these as implying that man is 'a leader and decision-maker' while woman is 'a loyal supporter and follower', and more recent evidence suggests that these ideas about men and women remain widespread.

Social roles

Via language, we clearly construct the sexes as separate and possessing different characteristics. However, this is not the only way in which our descriptions are gendered.

When we describe something, we often refer to its function and role: we talk of *wine* glasses and *dining* tables. The italic terms, or **modifiers**, are not just optional extra bits of information. They provide a detailed guide to the purpose of the objects: we are talking about glasses for wine as opposed to any other glasses (brandy glasses, cocktail glasses, sherry glasses, liqueur glasses) and a table for dining on (as opposed to a coffee table, a side table, an occasional table, a writing table). This kind of classification is very common in our everyday referencing system: we talk about *digital* files, *food* shops, *train* journeys.

Activity

As well as thinking about and expressing what objects are for, we also ascribe functions and roles to men and women: what are men and women for in society? To explore the way language can encode some of this information, look at the data in Text 2:1, which is from the front page of an American newspaper, *USA Today*.

* What types of information are given describing men and women?
* Are the types of information different and, if so, how?
* What functions, roles and relationships are being reported?
* How would you explain any differences you have found above?

Note that there is no commentary on this activity.

Text 2:1 *USA Today*

Descriptions of men and women on the front page of
***USA Today*, 9 May 2008**

Main stories: mortgage crisis; gas (petrol) costs rising; cigarettes being sold in fewer shops.
(Banner features a male sports figure, Sam Cassell, and a female singer, Jennifer Nettles.)

Men	**Women**
Sam Cassell	Jennifer Nettles
Brian Bethune of Global Insight	Wegmans spokeswoman
Assemblyman Sam Hoyt	Jo Natale
Dean Baker of the Centre for Economic & Policy Research	
Jeremy Brandt, CEO of 1-800-CashOffer	
San Francisco Mayor Gavin Newsom	
Bill Phelps, spokesman for Philip Morris USA	
Matt Myers, President of the Campaign for Tobacco-Free Kids	
Gary Nolan, national spokesman for Citizens Freedom Alliance	
Legendary singer Eddy Arnold	

Socialisation

To summarise so far, it is not difficult to find evidence for the idea that the language we use to talk about men and women is gendered. The way in which we talk about the sexes indicates that we possess a shared system of reference about traditional roles and about what is deemed masculine or feminine. First, we have sex-exclusive vocabulary – language that is used to describe *either* males *or* females (such as 'hunk' and 'buxom'). Second, we have language in which the linguistic item remains the same but the meaning changes according to whether it is men or women who are being described. Examples can cover physical attributes, as in the term 'well built', or behavioural traits, as in the term 'aggressive', which can have a positive meaning when applied to men (in sport, or in business contexts, for example) but has only a negative meaning when applied to women. Third, we present as salient *different* aspects of men and women (such as men as workers, women as mothers). We share an understanding about how men and women are meant to behave, and the characteristics they are meant to possess. This shared understanding is part of our **social knowledge**, that is, the frameworks or discourses we use to interpret the world – the understanding we have about how to operate in our environment; knowledge of the social rules that are part of our culture. This is not knowledge in the sense of facts or 'truth', but more a pragmatic awareness of how to function within society. We do not learn this knowledge explicitly, nor is it concrete and finite.

The process by which we acquire social knowledge and make it part of the way we think is called **socialisation**. This process is extensive and includes all the things we see and hear from society around us – the people we meet, the things we're told, the images we see, the books we read and so on. These sources also give us information about **identity** – who we are, and what being a man or woman means – because we learn about ourselves from the society around us. For example, Amy Paugh (2005) reported how overhearing and participating in parents' conversations about work during family dinners socialised children into 'the discourses and ideologies of work' and the 'work-related values and expectations' embedded in these discourses (p. 55).

The process of socialisation lasts our whole lifetime. We start to learn about the world from the moment we are born and it never stops – which is one of the reasons we can change our views, and why both society and language change. Learning about gender starts at a very early age. From birth onwards we are given certain types of toys, dressed in certain types of clothes, talked about and to in a certain way and told what behaviours are acceptable or not. As children we are bombarded with images that portray expectations about our future roles and preferences, with the sexes represented in very different ways. In other words, we quickly learn 'what we are for'. It is easy to think that the portrayal of girls and boys in traditional sex roles is no longer an acceptable or frequent occurrence. Unfortunately, this is far from true.

Activity

Look at the images in Text 2:2, taken from the children's catalogue of a popular US company.

• What male and female characteristics are being portrayed?

• What do the postures imply about the individuals?

• What connotations do the fabric patterns have?

• Now look at the names and descriptions for room décor and furnishings taken from recent catalogues. From Lists 1 and 2, which, if any, of the names and descriptions suggest that they are rooms for boys or for girls? Are any of them ambiguous and, if so, why?

Text 2:2 Children's catalogue images

List 1: Room décor names

Fairies and flowers	Ladybugfriends	In full bloom
Hiddentreasure	Team player	Camoflies
Saddle up	Crazy for daisies	Sharkbait

List 2: Décor names and extended descriptions

Room name	Extended description
A flair for fashion	Just the right mix of colors, fun and flowers to delight her
Fantasy in pink	Stylish and feminine, she'll love the fresh feeling of this big-girl room
Wild west bonanza	It's a round-up of great western décor to thrill any cowboy!
Let's play ball!	Create a classic haven for your sports fanatic
Fairy dust and fantasies!	Mirror, mirror on the floor. Your little princess will be the fairy-est of them all
Fit for a princess	Indulge her princess fantasies with our exclusive [name] furniture and adorable accents
Crazy 'bout sports	Spoil the sports enthusiast in your life with these unique gifts
Field of dreams	Solid, yet elegant, the [name] Collection offers a perfect stadium for the hopes, dreams and escapades of your football fanatic
His and Hers	Whether it's girl-time with Mommy or boy-time with Daddy, special moments happen here
Rub-a-dub-dub . . .	You'll stand a sporting chance of getting your boys in the tub when you add these fun accessories
Fresh as flowers	She'll look forward to getting clean in a bathroom filled with fresh colors

Commentary

In the images, you will notice that the girls are looking at each other, showing social affiliation, and standing in what is widely accepted as a submissive and passive pose (head is tilted to side and down, looking up at camera), while the boys are physically competing and standing in a power pose. These are very common gender **representational practices** observed in the media. You might also have noticed that all the girls are posed for the camera, while the arm-wrestling boys could have been caught in action (even though we know they are posing). The tendency to show females passively posing and males in action is a common practice that has been summarised by Berger (1972, p. 47) as '*men act* and *women appear*'. This suggests that men are often 'seen' doing and behaving, as if caught accidentally by the camera, while women are directly engaged with appearing for the camera and, therefore, for the audience as an object.

The room décor themes emphasise traditional gendered associations. These themes connect boys with outdoor physical activity and the girls with less active imaginations and aesthetics. Colour-coding is also an important symbol of gender. In the original catalogues the girls' rooms used lots of pink or other 'feminine' colours, such as pastels, while boys' rooms were often in darker, stronger colours, such as maroon, dark blue or dark green.

Early learning about sex differences provides a strong grounding for beliefs about which social roles are 'natural' to men and women. The greater presence of male characters and in more active roles in children's media is part of the learned pattern, but differences in voice-overs, narratives, language choices, voices and relations were all gendered features of television advertisements for children's toys identified by Johnson and Young (2002). However, the gendered portrayal of the sexes does not stop at childhood. Gender roles and preferences are reinforced by language and images throughout our lives: this means that they are persistently confirmed, maintained and strengthened. The strength of this learning is reflected in the extent to which masculine or feminine behaviours and preferences have become a completely 'natural' part of our identity by the time we reach adulthood, and continue to be seen as such: it's 'only natural' that Jane should like babies; it's 'only natural' that Jim should like football; Jane is 'naturally' better than Jim at ironing; Jim is 'naturally' better than Jane at building cupboards. And 'it's only natural' that they should get together, of course.

We can clearly see the idea of 'natural' male and female preferences in the ways consumer products are marketed. Many products are targeted at male or female consumers with the idea that the product is 'naturally' the province of one sex or the other. The language used about these products and the names given all serve to reinforce their femininity or masculinity. A prime example of this is cosmetics, which have been strongly associated with women and femininity for a long time. 'Real men' do not wear make-up – unless they're in army camouflage, drag or the Australian cricket team. So the language of cosmetic products such as lipstick, hair dye and nail varnish aimed at women often suggests a very traditional femininity, with ideas of delicacy and subtlety ('hint of a tint'), virginity and innocence ('peach blush') or the settings of popular romance novels, with their dreamy sunsets and pale heroines ('desert haze', 'white rose').

While face make-up is still exclusively targeted at women consumers, other cosmetic products (such as deodorants, fragrances, soaps, bath/shower gels) often have a male range as well as a female one. In these cases, it is interesting to see how the male product differs from the female one in how it is named and described. Sometimes, what is effectively exactly the same product is described very differently, to construct a distinctively different picture of the **narratee** (the person supposedly addressed by the text). For example, one company markets a face cleanser for men called 'scruffing solution', presumably hoping to capture the idea of vigorous activity along with a devil-may-care attitude in the word 'scruffing', and the idea of problem-solving in the word 'solution', as well as creating a scientific-sounding name overall. Added together, we have an active, carefree/rebellious, problem-solving, science-oriented narratee: not a bad profile for a 'real man' to aspire to.

Activity

Consider the language used in the advertisement for Aramis Lab Series For Men (Text 2:3).

*   What are the connotations of the names and descriptions?
*   What ideas about the male consumer are being suggested here?
*   How does the language used here differ from that of cosmetic products aimed at women?

Note that there is no commentary on this activity.

Text 2:3 Aramis advert

Fictional worlds

If the world is a gendered place in reality, this is likely to be reflected in fictive writing that is aiming for social realism. Such fiction, then, can be a good place to explore the ways in which language is gendered and to appreciate our ingrained beliefs about men and women. An added consideration is the power and status we ascribe to fiction: far from being a leisure pursuit that represents a minority interest, reading (or listening to and/or watching) stories represents a very common experience for all of us, and one that we appear to believe is very influential. If we didn't believe in the power of stories, then why have regulated and prescribed reading lists in school, why have endless debates on whether watching violent films is harmful, and why burn books and issue death threats to writers because of what they have put in a work of fiction?

The act of reading itself appears to be quite a gendered activity, with men and women habitually reading different kinds of books – women favouring romance and modern novels, and men favouring war, adventure and science fiction books, with the crime/thriller genre equally chosen by both sexes (Policy Studies Institute, 1989). But, as well as men and women having different domains in terms of genre, fiction books themselves regularly present men and women as distinctively different in behaviour and psychological traits.

Crossing the line between what we see as male and female domains in everyday life can startle us because it disrupts our habitual collocations: a woman in a jock-strap or a man in a flowery dress throw our expectations back into our faces, causing surprise, even shock. The fact that we notice a person because they are the 'wrong' sex can be seen as evidence of the gendered nature of the activity, behaviour or role.

Activity

Switching pronouns in a text is a disruptive strategy that can demonstrate the power of beliefs about gender roles and characteristics associated with masculinity and femininity. In Text 2:4, all the pronouns have been switched, so that previously male characters are now referred to as 'she' and previously female characters are now 'he'.

- How have these changes altered the way the characters are presented?

- What do the changes tell you about the way the text was previously gendered?

Note that there is no commentary on this activity.

35

Text 2:4 Switched pronouns

'You know what I'm talking about.' She was oddly elated, her eyes flashing down at him, her mouth curling at the edges with satisfaction.

Nervously he shook his head, the swing of his blonde hair against his cheek catching her eye. She shifted her hand to it, thrusting her fingers among the strands, winnowing them slowly and watching the way they drifted against her flesh.

'Don't lie to me, even if you've been lying to yourself.' Urgency deepened her voice and he felt a surge of panic begin inside him. 'Ever since I saw you at that window . . .'

'No!' he broke out, turning stumblingly away.

She pulled him back towards her, slamming him against her so abruptly that he fell, his face in her throat, his nostrils filling with the scent of her brown skin. Her hand gripped his back in a convulsive movement, the muscular tension of her body pressing against him.

'You looked fantastic. You're not ashamed of that are you? My God, you left me breathless!'

'Don't talk about it!' he begged.

'Why not, in God's name? For a second I thought you were a marble statue. It was the effect of the moonlight; you looked cool and remote and unreal. Then you moved and I felt as though someone had punched me in the stomach. You really knocked me out.'

He tried to pull away, trembling. 'Can't you see how embarrassing it is? I don't want to talk about it.'

'You're scared,' she whispered, her voice unsteady. 'Don't be. It's what you were born for, this feeling . . .'

'I just feel embarrassed,' he said angrily, struggling.

The elated excitement went out of her face and it darkened into impatience, her brows jerking together, her eyes staring at him with a glittering demand in them.

'That's not true. You just won't admit how you feel. Are you afraid of love?'

He threw caution to the wind, his temper hardening in his voice. 'You're not talking about love, you're talking about sex.'

'They're the same thing.'

(*Seduction,* Charlotte Lamb, pp. 64–5)

Fictionalising ourselves

It's easy to look at published works of fiction, and decide that genderised descriptions of men and women are what other people do – but not us. The introduction to this unit suggested that we all 'do' gender on a daily basis, and this means all of us, not just people who create those texts that society considers important or powerful. The final activity in this unit will focus on some texts that anybody can write, and will explore the extent to which gender affects the way we fictionalise ourselves.

Activity

Social networking sites such as MySpace and Facebook have been seen as places where we are constantly constructing our identities, often on a daily basis. Chandler (1997) suggests that this work is never finished – that our identities are permanently 'under construction' as we change and adapt the way our sites look.

Read through the data in Text 2:5, which shows extracts from the 'Personal Info' sections of three individuals' Facebook pages.

*   What impression do you get of each person's identity?

*   Do the writers of the texts present a certain kind of masculine or feminine identity? If so, what aspects of language contribute to those impressions?

Note that there is no commentary on this activity, but the sex of each writer is revealed at the end of the unit.

Text 2:5 Facebook

Facebook 'Personal Info' Sections

Person A:

Interests: I like the odd drink of vodka, shots, wine, archers, alcopops . . . often in quite large quantities on the same night! But hey your only young once! :-p I love to dance the night away! I love to cuddle (especially if it's with a certain person . . .). I like to sing loudly and badly . . . (well that's debatable) . . . I think I'm a brilliant singer!

Favourite Music: Hm I'm a pretty mixed bag in this department :-p . . . I like RnB and Dance for nights out coz they're great to dance to! I like a bit of the old cheesy pop . . . but who doesn't! A bit of arctic monkeys, fratellis, muse etc doesn't go amiss these days either!

Person B:

Favourite Music:	pretty varied
Favourite Movies:	one flew over the cuckoos nest
	face/off
	old school
	starsky and hutch!!!!!
Favourite Books:	on the road
About Me:	i love vimto

Person C:

Activities:	I like bits of everything, whatever comes up, il do
Favorite Music:	Im a gangsta at heart, lol! Love RnB and hip hop but everyone has their geeky moments and puts something stupid on
Favorite TV Shows:	Ive recently realised that im obbsessed with the simpsons
Favorite Movies:	I used to be rubbish at films before i came to uni and got bullied into watching the greats. Pulp fiction, lock stock, layer cake, snatch
Favorite Books:	Books, what are they? Not a great reader but there have been a few that have taken me back (and i don't mean harry potter)
Favorite Quotes:	The difference between success and failure is hanging on when others let go (some gangstars told me and it kinda stuck)
About Me:	Not much to tell, i like to try everything once

Summary

This unit has had as its focus the qualities and attributes that women and men are expected to have, and the way in which we circulate these expectations via language and images in many different contexts.

Extension activities

1 Make a collection of terms that you think tend to be used more of one sex than another. If possible, collect terms in context – that is, in use in texts such as newspapers, magazines, adverts, novels, radio and TV programmes, casual conversation, oral stories and jokes. For spoken texts, write down a record of the term within the utterance where it occurred. Note who was speaking and the context of the conversation and, in the case of a broadcast text, details of the programme's content, channel and timing. Also collect terms that you think can be used of either sex, but which tend to mean something different when used of one sex or the other.

   When you have collected more than a dozen terms, try them out on some informants, by repeating the activity you did on page 25 of this unit.

2 Collect some examples of how men and women are referred to in the press or in TV or radio news broadcasts, during one day's news coverage. Choose for your focus two contrasting papers or channels in terms of their ideology/political persuasion.

3 Analyse some toy and clothes catalogues for children. What colours are being used and what types of clothing and activities are represented? Look carefully at the verbal language, including brand names, descriptions, slogans and logos. What sex roles are being portrayed? What skills would be learned by the children who played with these toys?

   Focus on one particular type of toy – for example, bicycles – and, looking at the pages where bikes are displayed, see if you can spot which bikes are for girls and which for boys.

4 Select some television shows designed for toddlers. Count the number of male and female characters and describe their characteristics and activities. Where do they fit into the narrative? Are they heroic, action-oriented problem solvers or are they socially caring and supportive problem solvers? What are they good at and what can't they do? What sorts of voices and music are used?

5   Collect some brand names and descriptions of cosmetic products aimed at adult men and women. Do they differ? If so, how? What constructions are being offered of the target audience in each case?

6   Focus on a particular genre of literary or film fiction and analyse the ways in which male and female characters are portrayed. You can learn a lot about the approach of a book or film just from its title and 'blurb' alone. If you list as many titles as you can find for a particular genre – for example, horror novels or films – you will soon get a sense of the concerns and outlook promoted by that genre. Film posters and trailers are especially revealing. You could also look at changes in the portrayal of such characters over time.

7   Look out particularly for texts that play around with the idea of gender, or that overturn traditional ideas. For example, there are now many women writers of detective fiction who have a female 'sleuth'. You could compare some of these figures with their conventional male counter-parts. You could also investigate texts that deliberately shift perspectives, such as Virginia Woolf's *Orlando* (1928), which has a narrator who changes sex, or the film *I'm Not There* (2007), which used different actors, one of whom was a female, to play the famous (male) musician Bob Dylan. Sometimes, writers have narrators who are a different sex from themselves – for example, Martin Amis has a female detective narrator (called 'Mike Hoolihan') in *Night Train* (1997), and Peter Hoeg does the same in *Miss Smilla's Feeling for Snow* (1995). Are these convincing? Do you think it is possible for people of one sex to write as another?

8   Collect some data from social networking sites (SNS) and explore the extent to which users appear to be constructing particular masculinities and femininities.

9   Try to write a description of a person that does not use gendered language or subscribe to traditional sex roles. Extend this to include some action.

Commentaries/Answers to activities

ANSWER: ACTIVITY p. 37, TEXT 2:5

Person A is female, B is male, C is female.

All in the mind?

In this unit the relationship between thought and language, introduced in Unit one, is considered in more depth, in order to explore the thinking and associated language features involved in **stereotyping** and **marking**.

We can all think about something, but *how* we think and reason is more mysterious. The way our minds work is strongly related to our language and our culture, because it is through these that we perceive and understand the 'real world'. To appreciate this relationship it is necessary to consider some ideas about how the brain functions in relation to the world and language, and how language influences the way our brains organise information.

You will already have noticed that the two terms 'brain' and 'mind' have been used interchangeably above. In fact, these two terms have often been used historically to mean different things, and there are still many debates on how they differ. For example, 'brain' has often been used to denote biological and functional activities (such as movement, speech production and memory), while 'mind' has often included more individual, creative and imaginative aspects of mental activity (such as dreaming and thinking). There isn't space to enter this debate here, but it's important to mention that you will come across these terms in some academic traditions (such as that of psychology) as representing different things. However, in this book, we will be using the terms interchangeably.

41

The language of the mind

Thinking, memory, reasoning, perception and other psychological pro-cesses that occur in the brain are referred to as aspects of **cognition**. Cognitive processes are involved in every aspect of how we interact with the world – how and what we perceive, understand and decide, and how we behave.

As far as we know, cognitive structures and processes do not *physically* exist, unlike biological or physiological structures and processes. There are parts of the brain that we know are associated with certain types of cognitive activity, such as speech or sight, but how these actually function remains unclear. For example, when we 'see' and 'hear', we do something fairly amazing with the signals we receive from the world. Very simply, seeing involves signals in the form of light hitting parts of the eye, which causes cells in the eye to react (or **fire**) in a way that sets off a chain of cell reaction up the optic nerve and into the brain. In the brain, our cognitive processes transform the firing of cells (**neurones**) into recognisable visual information – shapes, depth, size, colour, people, objects, movement, etc. This transformation into 'real' information occurs in a miniscule amount of time. Imagine if cognitive processes took so long that there was a perceivable delay between 'seeing' something and 'knowing' that you could see it. Trying to touch an object in front of us would be difficult, especially if it was moving, walking would be hazardous and driving would be lethal.

As we can't physically 'get to' our cognitive processes, we only have theories about how they work, based upon the evidence provided by data – our everyday experiences of thinking, talking, dreaming and imagining – as well as scientific studies. There are specific areas of the brain that we know are involved in understanding and producing language, but we still don't know *how* language is understood or stored. In fact, we know very little about the brain as a whole, especially compared to the knowledge we have of other processes and structures, such as the heart and lungs and how oxygen and carbon dioxide are exchanged in the bloodstream.

Activity

The aim of this activity is to get you to think about how we think about thinking! The particular focus is to explore the idea that the ways we think, or conceptualise, are based upon the language that we have and the culture that we are in.

Look at the terms below, which are all ways that we talk about our brains. All the terms are **metaphors**, which are ways of talking about something in terms of something else. The terms in the first group are older than those in the second group.

- What are the two sets of metaphors based on?
- Why do you think we use metaphorical language to talk about our brains?
- Does it make any difference which metaphors we use to describe ourselves? Should we really be using metaphors at all?

Group 1	Group 2
I can't get my brain into gear	My memory is full
I'm only firing on two cylinders	Let me process the information
I'm a bit rusty	I'm in active mode today
I need to get the cogs turning	I need to switch off for a minute

Commentary

Both sets of metaphors are based upon the idea of the brain as a machine, but the first group is based on 'old' technology and the second group on 'new' technology such as computers. Neither group of terms describes anything real in the sense of describing what our brains are really doing: metaphors are forms of figurative language that we often use when we want to turn something abstract into something concrete and understandable. For example, we often talk about our emotions, which are also abstract entities, in metaphorical terms, such as 'I really boiled over', 'I had steam coming out of my ears' or 'I exploded', when we talk about anger. Some linguists, for example George Lakoff (1987), maintain that most of our everyday language is in fact metaphorical.

Although these phrases seem 'real' to us, they are just one way of representing the world to ourselves, and they are culture-specific. It is no accident that we now talk about our brains as if they were computers, since this new technology is so pervasive, and especially since scientists themselves have been using the computer as a model for the brain for some time. Scientific discourses are no more 'real' than any others, despite their persuasive power in society.

But imagine that our society was all focused on horticulture – we might talk about our brains in the following ways:

I can't think, I need fertilising
I have ideas budding
My brain needs pruning
I need repotting

If we described ourselves as plants instead of machines, we might see ourselves quite differently. For example, we might expect our brains to be quite dormant for part of the year, and to become more active in the 'growing season'.

The main points to carry forward from this exercise are that:
- abstract ideas and processes – such as thinking – are often described metaphorically, because they are hard to 'get at';
- if we look at the language used to describe something, we can gain an understanding of the way that thing is being conceptualised by the members of that culture;
- concepts are not 'real' (although they seem so), but are constructed using social experience and discourses;
- our concepts produce consequences for us.

Cognition and language

Language and linguistic knowledge are cognitive components, just like memory and imagination. However, language actually plays a very important and fundamental role in cognition because language influences the way in which we organise our cognitive system – this means that language influences the way the brain organises thought and knowledge. This is why some people believe that cognition plays an important role between discourses and the social world; that cognition is the 'interface' between discourses and society (van Dijk, 1993, p. 251).

Like all large masses of knowledge (such as libraries, computers, etc.) the brain has a system of organisation to enable the location, retrieval and use of the information it contains. The basis of the brain's cognitive system is categories and, since categories are labelled linguistically, this means that language influences our thinking and reasoning via the process of categorisation.

Why do we categorise?

The world is a highly complex place. So many things happen in it at one time that it is impossible to comprehend everything. In cognitive terms this means that we cannot process all the information or data that we are receiving from our senses at the same time – even the data just from our eyes or ears is too much. To enable us to function and understand what is happening in the world, we need to both simplify and become selective about what information gets processed and how far it gets processed, that is, what gets processed to the extent that we notice it, pay attention to it and consciously think about it.

Categorising allows us to generate 'everyday' thinking that is automatic, quick and effortless, without which interacting with the world would become a long and laborious process. Categories exist for everything – people, objects, events, emotions, language components, etc. When we come across something unknown we make an effort to find out information that enables us to categorise it so we can understand what it is.

Activity

Imagine a situation in which you have come across an object that you cannot recognise – you have no idea what it is or what it does. What questions might you ask about it? Can you think of a question you might ask that does not seek to categorise the object?

Now think about how you might explain an unknown object or phenomenon to another person – such as snow or a car or a dress. Can you do it without referring to the categories it belongs to? If you are describing a cultural artefact, can you do it without referring to other cultural values and discourses? For example, how would you explain the very British phenomenon, 'Page 3' (of *The Sun* newspaper), to people from other cultures (you can go to www.thesun.co.uk to get a sense of this), or the American phenomenon of 'cheerleading'?

45

Commentary

The process of categorisation involves the grouping together of 'things' that are related. This means that we must have some basis for believing these things to be related – a concept or **cognitive model** that puts these things together in a group. In this way, a linguistic category also embodies a cognitive model. So, with reference to the previous items, linguistic categories of types of weather conditions, types of vehicle and types of clothing all embody cognitive models, in which there are shared ideas or understandings that we tend to take for granted.

Keeping it simple

'Everyday' thinking and language use simplified category models – a few 'rules of thumb' to serve as a cognitive 'short cut'. Unfortunately, simplifying also means having to lose information and make general assumptions, which means the loss of individual detail. We simplify using social knowledge. This means that cultural values and beliefs provide the basis for the simplifications and general rules embodied in cognitive models, even if we 'know' that things are not really that simple. For example, traditional 'stick figures' representing men and women use a skirt and long hair to denote female. We know that the reality of women with long hair and skirts is no longer a true reflection of society – but we understand the concepts being represented and who the symbols represent. It is such shared cognitive models that allow us to use non-word symbols as representations of categories.

Activity

The symbols in Text 3:1 have all been used to represent men and women, many of them on toilet doors. Look at the symbols, decide which represents the man or the woman, and then discuss what cognitive models or cultural concepts they embody (that is, what shared social knowledge is encoded).

46

Text 3:1 Symbols

Commentary

You might have realised that some of the symbols only work when used with another matched symbol or label, for instance the glasses. One of the pairs of symbols is from Poland and, unless you are Polish, you may have found it harder to decide which is male or female, and why: the circle and triangle are the Polish symbols for women and men, respectively. It is unclear how Polish people 'rationalise' these symbols: one piece of anecdotal evidence given to us by a group of Polish teachers was that 'men have broad shoulders and women are rounded'. You might also note the different stances and other nuances (such as the cherry in the cocktail glass) and consider the variety of implicit ideas about masculinity and femininity embodied in these symbols.

You may also wonder where the familiar male and female symbols of the circle with an arrow or cross come from. Wikipedia reports that these come from symbols for the planets. The female sign is for Venus – the Roman goddess of love – and is described as 'a hand mirror symbolising beauty'. The male sign is for Mars – the Roman god of war – and is described as being adapted from the symbol for Venus, but using an arrow to make it resemble a shield and spear. This explanation itself reveals the interconnectedness of the gendered understandings embedded in the symbolism used to name, categorise and define the planets, the gods and their signs. The oppositionally gendered symbolism of Mars and Venus continues to be adopted to popularise ideas about supposed differences in speech styles and conversational intent between males and females. These ideas are considered further in Unit five.

There are also verbal labels that only work properly in context, or that play writing off against speech. For example, the following denoting of men's and women's toilets has been observed in seaside restaurants with nautical themes: inboard and outboard motors; buoys (pronounced 'boys' in Britain) and gulls. But there are many types of gender coding, colour being another common and powerful form.

Constructing categories

Categories, especially social categories, actually only exist because they are viewed as culturally significant. A category can also only exist in contrast with something else, that is it would not exist if there was no alternative. For example, if there was only one sex then there would be no sex categories. Equally, if race was not significant politically then the use of the categories of 'black' and 'white' would not be used to refer to or describe people. This may sound a bit odd, that such apparently obvious perceptual or biological distinctions as male or female, masculine or feminine and black or white might not be made. But the categories that are used in a society are a reflection of what the society *believes* to be important about people; beliefs that are based upon its political and social order – its **ideology**.

Support for the idea that categories reflect culture rather than 'physical reality' has been provided by cross-cultural studies. Evidence shows that, if a category is not socially important, it is not used to describe or differentiate people. This also means that any category could become important depending upon the beliefs a society develops. For example, if 'handedness' was a significant social category, this would be used to distinguish people. In fact, in the past, this was an important category: left-handedness was once viewed as evil and a 'sign of the devil', and even in more recent times left-handed schoolchildren had their left hands tied behind their backs so that they would have to write with their right hand.

Even when a category such as gender is shared by most cultures, it does not mean that there are shared discourses or attitudes towards that category. This means that the cognitive model embodied in a shared category can vary between cultures. The idea that women are not suited to doing 'heavy work' is only relevan[t] ... cultures where women are seen as physically weaker. In so... ...men do the heavy work that is often considered ... Britain and the USA. However, this does not n... ...ssarily view men and women as equal. In fact ... e, with women doing heavy, unskilled work b... ...lly inferior.

Such eviden... ...hink is socially constructed, that is, based upo... ...er relations rather than a literal representation ... d its 'natural order'. This extends to many conc... ...he world and the way we live within it. For example, t... ...at 'time is money' is a metaphor based upon Western concepts of work, financial profit and financial reward. Even apparently basic concepts, such as time and the way it moves, vary across societies and cultures. The notion that time moves forward – that there is a past, present and future – or that it is divided into hours, minutes and seconds is not shared by all cultures.

The power of cognitive models

Even though cognitive models are very simplified constructions of the world, they contain a tremendous amount of information and have a powerful impact on the way we think, yet most of the time we are unaware of them: how often do you actually consider what 'time' is, how it moves and what we mean when we say things like 'I haven't got time', 'time flies' or 'we've run out of time'?

The power of cognitive models comes from the fact that we take them for granted. We learn them through socialisation and language acquisition so that social knowledge is mainly integrated into the ways we think without us being aware. For example, in Britain we don't tend to think of 'rat', 'horse' or 'insect' as members of the food category, but there are parts of the world where these items are considered delicacies. In the same way, some cultures regard the eating of pork as disgusting, the eating of beef as sacrilegious or the idea of consuming meat at all as abhorrent. Food is an area where cultural norms and social values can strongly influence what we think of as fitting the category, and where cognitive models vary enormously across cultures. Models also vary through time. For example, a great delicacy in Tudor Britain was the swan; nowadays, we are more likely to feed them bread than stuff them with it for the oven.

It is the embodiment of cultural concepts in the cognitive model, and hence language, that underlies the reason why language is not neutral – because *attitudes and beliefs are part of the cognitive model.* The cognitive model embodied in a category is usually obvious to the members of the society or culture – so obvious it does not even need to be consciously thought about. It is only when a cognitive model does not fit with the situation that we tend consciously to pay attention and 'think about it'; that is, when the object, event or situation is not typical. This is a bit like seeing a three-legged dog; we tend to notice it because in our cognitive model dogs have four legs. A 'typical' dog is the cognitive model.

The influence of beliefs or suppositions is apparent in the once famous 'taste-test' challenge between the two leading cola brands. Over the years studies have consistently shown that, when the containers of cola are not labelled, most people prefer the less popular brand. But, when the containers are labelled, but all contain the same cola, most people select as their preference the cola labelled as the most popular brand. Such findings consistently suggest that pre-existing knowledge and associations influence expectations and perception. This susceptibility is why the marketing and advertising industries have become very interested in exploiting the connection between language, (brand) knowledge, emotions and perception, an area increasingly known as **neuromarketing**. Of course, whether we think we like one brand of cola rather than another isn't really that important. But understanding the extent to which existing ideas and suppositions can influence how we perceive and understand, and why it may be so hard for us to think in different ways, is important for society; especially if we are concerned about issues of equality. This is explored more in Unit four.

Typicality

Although categories appear to be quite simple things, the way they work is actually quite complex. For a start, categories are not clear-cut and exclusive; instead they often share members and have sub-categories. There are also category members (**hyponyms**) that we think of as more typical or more central than other members. The central members are those that fit the cognitive model or category best, and these are the basis for our idea of 'the **norm**'. For example, when the category 'bird' is mentioned most people think of a robin or a sparrow – rather than a penguin or a chicken – because robins and sparrows fit our norm model of a bird more precisely. These members are said to have central status in the category.

Activity

To explore the nature of categories and their group members, look at the data in the table below.

For each group, try to arrive at a rank order for which of the group members is the best example of that category, then at the bottom of the list put the group member that least fits into that category.

When you have finished, try to explain your rationale for the rank order you have established for each group.

Pets	Birds	Parts of the body	Furniture	Vehicles	Adverts
dog	ostrich	hair	chair	car	branded carrier bag
spider	finch	head	stool	bicycle	TV commercial
cat	seagull	leg	table	skate-board	film trailer
snake	turkey	fingers	lamp	truck	university prospectus

Commentary

There is no right or wrong answer to this activity. The point is to think about how your cognitive models affected the way in which you assessed the group members. For example, if your concept of 'birdiness' excludes edibility, then

51

you will have put the turkey at the bottom (but note that finches are also eaten in some cultures, as is ostrich); if 'birdiness' for you is strongly about flight and small size, then ostrich will be low on the list and finch high.

Some other rank orders might relate to ideas about dependency and secondary status: for example, hair is attached to the head, so 'hair' might seem dependent or secondary to the more important group member, 'head'. In the same way, a lamp sits on a table and a stool could be seen as a chair with the back missing, so lamp and stool could be seen as secondary in these cases. It all depends on how you conceptualise the items.

Central status is not necessarily about items that are typical because they are common in our own experience; it is more about the fact that they distil a number of qualities that we see as essential to the definition, and, for this reason, are at the basis of frequent cultural representations. For example, you may never have seen a finch in reality, but the idea of a small, fluttery, pretty creature that sings attractively may fit your concept of 'birdiness' better than the lumbering, noisy, rather unappealing turkey or ostrich. And, for this very reason, people who want to suggest 'birdiness' in visual texts may choose that particular bird a lot, so that we think it is common and typical. You can see this process operating with the robin, who turns up unfailingly on British Christmas cards as a stocky, cheeky little creature with a red breast.

The cognitive models that represent these 'typical' or 'central' members are called **prototypes**, and it is usually prototypical models that come to mind when a category is called up. This means that prototypes can often represent the whole category in our thinking.

From prototypical to stereotypical

As well as categorising objects, we also categorise people into groups where some group members are seen as more typical or representative than others, even though in reality they may be in the minority. When we construct a simplified and limited model from the characteristics of a few group members and apply these to the whole group, what we are doing is stereotyping. Stereotypes are often exaggerated, composite pictures that share many of the qualities of caricature. Stereotyping is very much about the process of applying a simplified model to a real, complex individual, often to negative and derogatory effect. So, forms of 'cognitive short-hand' or 'rules of thumb', which are useful to us in other ways in order to simplify the world, become applied as sets of very restricting general-isations that suppress individual complexity. Stereotypes gain power and credibility through wide use in everyday talk and texts as a result of the fact that they are 'well understood or easy to perceive' (Lakoff, 1987, p. 77), rather than because they are true. Obviously, this is not just a psychological process that operates in a vacuum: our stereotypes are very bound up with the social and political structures of our culture. This can be seen in the cartoon in Text 3:2, which relies for its effect on a number of social stereotypes.

Text 3:2 Brain cartoon

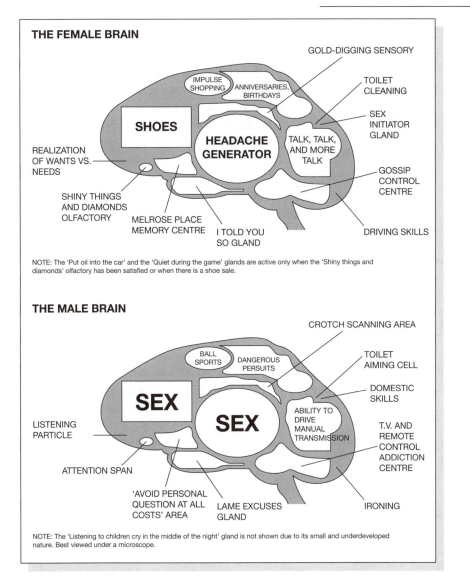

Commentary

This cartoon uses the common belief that men's and women's brains are different, yet there is little evidence to support the idea of a consistent and real difference. Humour often uses familiar stereotypes and ideas because they are shared, easily recognised cultural material, making them ideal for reaching a wide audience quickly. This is also why stereotypes are a familiar part of advertising. But, just because they can be funny or quickly understood, it doesn't make them accurate or true.

Many people will tell you that there must be a kernel of truth in stereotypes because 'there is no smoke without fire'. But, like smoke from an artificial smoke machine, stereotypes can be based upon misconceptions and false beliefs. They are also so simple and broad that there is bound to be one aspect that fits *everybody* – so they can appear to work when we apply them. And, of course, we should ask where the stereotype comes from, what it achieves, and in whose interests it is to maintain it. For example, there are statistics that show that many women shop more than men, but really it depends on what you define as shopping. Many shopping statistics focus on food and other 'household' shopping for families, which is often done by women. Food shopping is an activity that is a product of historical practices of gendered domestic labour division. But, if shopping includes cars, CDs, iTunes, etc., do we still think of women as 'the shoppers'?

Mark my words

The whole process of categorising, with its reliance on typicality, is very strongly connected with how linguistic items are marked in various ways in order to indicate what is 'normal' and what is **deviant**.

The first point to make is that marking can be covert as well as overt: that is, linguistic meanings can derive as much from their structural relationships as from the specific markings that occur on the words themselves. The activities that follow will illustrate these different aspects.

There are many pairs of terms in English that act as **antonyms**, where one term is unmarked and the other marked. The unmarked term is the term that would be used in straightforward questions and statements, while the marked term reflects an unusual or particular meaning. So, for example, in the pair of terms to describe age – 'old' and 'young' – the unmarked term is 'old' in the following:

How old are you?

If you used the term 'young' in the same structure, the implied meaning would be very different – not a straightforward question about age, but a question in which the youth of the interlocutor has already been established:

How young are you?

Now read through the antonyms in the sentences below. Decide which is the unmarked and which the marked term in each case. Also decide what the marked term might be implying, by describing a context in which the marked example might occur:

How tall are you?
How short are you?
How heavy is that parcel?
How light is that parcel?
How fast does this car go?
How slow does this car go?
How big is the pay rise going to be?
How small is the pay rise going to be?
Can you think of any further pairs of words that act in the same way?

Note that there is no commentary on this activity.

This activity will familiarise you with more overt linguistic marking, in the form of modification. Think about the ordinary term 'mother'. Write down what you see as its denotation and connotations. When you have done this, read through the terms below and decide, for each one, how the addition of a descriptive item alters the image of the mother being represented:

working mother	surrogate mother	stepmother
foster-mother	godmother	biological mother
adoptive mother	single mother	housemother (a woman with a pastoral role in a school – usually a public school*)

Commentary

The markings in each of the phrases above are used to tell us that the label departs from some unstated 'norm' or typical situation. Often it is very useful to examine marked items as a way to get back to what is at the basis of the unmarked term.

For example, the phrase 'working mother' suggests that the norm for 'mother' is someone who stays at home to look after the children and does not have paid employment. (One question often asked wryly about the literal meaning of the phrase 'working mother' is: Is there any other kind?) The phrase 'single mother' tells us that the 'ideal' is marriage or partnership.

Other phrases above appear to deviate from an idea of 'naturalness' that is to do with a combination of two factors: being a biological parent, and nurturing and caring for a child. In each case above, one of these two factors is missing. So a godmother, stepmother, foster-mother, housemother and adoptive mother may all look after a child's welfare, but they are not the child's biological parent. A surrogate mother and biological mother have biological connections, but the implications are that this is the point where it ends.

So the unmarked term 'mother' can be seen as representing a norm of: staying at home, not being in paid employment, being in a relationship, being the biological parent and nurturing and caring for the child. You could, therefore, say that 'mother' is our unmarked term that represents a kind of default model – that is, the meaning we return to if no other marking is present.

Activity

What do the following marked expressions on the right tell us about the meaning of the unmarked term on the left? In turn, what does the existence of all these pairs of terms tell us about the relationship between gender and the social and political structures of our society?

* British term for private school.

nurse	male nurse
prostitute	male prostitute
doctor	woman doctor
priest	woman priest
secretary	male secretary
model	male model
boy	toy boy
girl	career girl

Commentary

Increasingly, terms are being used that are supposedly gender neutral, such as flight attendant, police officer and firefighter. But who comes to mind when these terms are used still reflects embedded knowledge from discourses and ideology about gender and jobs.

Activity

There are other forms of marking that are more clearly part of the **morphological** system of English, for example **suffixes** such as 'ess' and 'ette'. We have pairs of terms where the unmarked form is male, and the marked form female. Not only does this suggest that the male figure is the 'norm' and the female one 'deviant', but the female form clearly has derived status and, in the case of 'ette', implies diminution or imitation (cigarette is a small cigar, suedette is 'false' suede). Read through the pairs below and say whether you think the words in each pairing have equal value in terms of the social status of their referents.

manager	manageress
usher	usherette
actor	actress
god	goddess
lad	ladette
waiter	waitress
mayor	mayoress
master	mistress

Note that there is no commentary on this activity.

Cognition and reference

This final section will look at the idea of **generic** and **sex-specific reference** in terms of our thinking and language use. Later in the section we will be concentrating on pronouns, but to start with we will look at the distribution of the terms 'man/boy' and 'woman/girl' in everyday phrases and sayings in English. A common theme for the whole section is how we refer to people when we don't want to name them specifically, but just suggest a hypothetical male or female figure.

Text 3:3 Lost consonants

Graham Rawle's **LOST CONSONANTS**

© Graham Rawle 1990

— — CUT OUT AND COLLECT THE SERIES

(70) **One of man's earliest inventions was the heel**

Fill in the missing word or word-parts in the phrases below and think about what they mean and why they are so familiar to us. Can you think of any other phrases or idioms that reflect our societal concepts of gendered work, domestic roles and appropriate social behaviour?

Because these sayings are so familiar, it might help you to turn them round when you have filled them in, by making them apply to the opposite sex, and think about the effect of the changes you have made. Many of the phrases below are using man/boy or woman in a sex-specific sense: in other words, the intended meaning is 'male people' or 'female people'. But, in some cases, it could be argued that 'man' is being used generically – that is, to suggest 'people in general'. What do you think?

A _____ place is in the home

It's a _____ world

May the best _____ win

Chair _____ of the Board

_____ will be _____

That's no job for a _____

Best _____ for the job

One of the _____

Take it like a _____

The old _____ network

Note that there is no commentary on this activity.

Now read through the phrases below, and think about the following questions.

•   What pictures are created in your mind as you process the meaning of each example? For example, do you 'see' men, women or both sexes?

•   Which of the phrases are most strongly sex-specific? Are there any that work generically?

59

Neanderthal man

Man breastfeeds his young

Man and machine in perfect harmony

Of mice and men

Man needs food, water and shelter to survive

A small step for a man, a giant leap for mankind

If man was meant to fly he'd have been given wings

An Englishman's home is his castle

A gentleman's agreement

Man overboard

A man-made environment

A man's best friend is his dog

The man in the street

The average working man

Note that there is no commentary on this activity.

Gender, generics and grammatical rules

Sometimes, when writers use the term 'gender' in talking about grammar, they are referring to the way some languages give nouns a specific gender, which is marked structurally. For example, in German, the word for 'lamp' – *die Lampe* – is female, while the word for 'table' – *der Tisch* – is male. These categories bear no relation to the idea of gender as we are using the term here. However, our idea of gender and the subject of grammar are strongly connected in another way, and that is the ruling of early English grammarians that the noun 'man' and the pronoun 'he' should be used not only to refer to men but also for general reference, to refer to 'all persons'. Their justification for this rule was that it represented the natural order of things:

> Some will set the Carte before the horse, as thus. My mother and my father are both at home, even thoughe the good man of the house ware no breaches or that the graye Mare were the better Horse. And what thoughe it often so happeneth (God wotte the more pitte) yet in speaking at the leaste, let us kepe a natural order, and set the man before the woman for maners Sake.
>
> (Wilson, 1560, p. 189, cited in Bodine, 1975, p. 128)

60

This grammatical rule was the subject of British parliamentary legislation in 1850, and has been handed down to us via rules of 'correct' usage in grammar books. One result of this is that we have had a long history of seeing certain usages as good or bad, right or wrong English simply in terms of grammatical rules, rather than as good or bad language in terms of how people were represented or referred to in communication and thinking. Also, grammatical rules are one thing, but real English is another. People have regularly used 'they' as a way of getting round the pronoun problem when speaking, even in formal contexts. For example, in the UK, here is what you hear on the telephone if you dial 1471 to find out who has phoned you and the caller has left no 'trace':

> You were called today at [time]. The caller withheld *their* number.

In terms of traditional grammatical rules, the sentence above has been seen historically as incorrect because the plural 'they' is being coupled with the singular noun 'caller'. However, it has more often been in written rather than spoken usage that contestations have arisen. And, even now, with our modern acceptance of the need for change, supposedly sex-generic 'he'/'his' and 'man' are more likely to crop up in official written documents and institutional discourse than elsewhere. The problem is that such discourse very much has the stamp of authority and 'truth'.

Generics and cognition

From a social psychological and cognitive perspective, the crux of the issue should not be about what is grammatically 'correct', particularly since grammatical rules are 'man-made'. Instead, the issue should be about who is represented in thought when these terms are actually used – that is, who is represented cognitively.

Studies have shown that generic usage does not readily invoke a generic meaning – that is, using 'he' or 'him' and 'man' or 'men' in neutral contexts results in most people thinking of a man (e.g. Khosroshahi, 1989). 'They' has been found to more readily suggest a mixture of both men and women, although 'he/she' and 'humans' comes out best at ensuring people think about women as well. Even in cases where we 'know' that 'man' is meant generically, we still tend to think 'male'. This is because the unmarked form is male, which means that we immediately and automatically think male until we realise it's meant to be generic. Even then, a generic reading is a secondary reading, and this fact has important implications for us cognitively, not least because additional cognitive processing or effort is required for the generic usage to be perceived and then understood.

This secondary processing of the generic meaning may seem relatively trivial if we just take into account the miniscule amount of time it actually takes to perceive a generic meaning as opposed to a male-specific reading. However, cognitively and socially the impact of this first male reading has important implications – because it means we think male unless context or linguistic marking suggests otherwise. The problem with context as an indication of generic intent is that, too often, the reading can be both specific and generic. This means that there are many instances in which an intended generic reading will be missed as the male-specific reading makes sense (since this is processed first and the secondary reading will only occur if no sense can be made). For example, 'best man for the job', can easily be read as male-specific, so any intended generic reading can disappear. The force of male-specific reading is well illustrated in the slogan that was carried on a march in Paris by women wanting to remind people that half the population was female:

One in two men is a woman.

Many men thought this was a statement that was questioning their masculinity.

So why do male pronouns and other supposedly generic terms auto-matically invoke male cognitive models? As children, the first members of a category that we learn are usually the prototypes – the models that will dominate our thinking in unmarked contexts. In the case of male pronouns and other generic terms, we learn their sex-specific meaning long before we learn their potentially generic meaning. This means that the male-specific meaning is the prototype.

Some researchers have claimed that the use of male terms in supposedly generic contexts functions to exclude women from language, rendering them 'cognitively invisible' (Ng, 1990) – that is, it excludes them from thought. But, although they can 'disappear' in generic contexts, female figures clearly do feature in texts via specifically female references such as the pronoun 'she'.

The debate about grammar, language choices and who gets repre-sented and how has led to some significant changes in recommended language use, with the wide adoption of gender-neutral choices in generic contexts. Examples of this noted above were the use of plural language (their) for singular generic contexts and neutral naming terms, such as police officer. This is sometimes referred to as 'politically correct' language, which is the topic of the next unit. But using gender neutral language does not guarantee generic comprehension. Singular gender neutral usage (their) can be primarily understood as plural, and neutral naming terms can still evoke gender-specific ideas (i.e. thinking male when the term police officer is used). This is because dominant discourses and stereotypes provide frames of reference or context for comprehension that undercut neutral language usage, making it redundant or simply lip-service.

Summary

This unit has provided more information about the ways in which our language is far from neutral. Although the relationship is complex, you should now have some understanding of the way in which language embodies our cultural, social and ideological values and the way we invoke these automatically in our thinking. It should be clear that language is not a direct reflection of any natural order, but a daily enactment of a social one. This means that, when we speak, we don't just say words, we speak our culture. This idea will be taken up again in the next unit on 'Political correctness'.

Extension activities

1   Investigate the way symbols work in computer contexts.

    (a)   The symbols below, for example, represent the email inbox in America, but not in Britain. Why do you think this is so?

    (b)   What other metaphorical uses can you find in computer-mediated communication systems you are familiar with, and why are they used? Can you detect any culture that is especially dominant when it comes to providing metaphors for such systems?

2   Research to what extent people picture typical figures for certain occupations. You could do this by asking people to describe the ideal characteristics of the occupants of some chosen jobs, such as the following:

Police officer	Car mechanic	Lawyer	Chef
Soldier	Beautician	Journalist	Cook
Childminder	Gardener	Surgeon	Engineer
Farmer	Midwife	Priest	Computer programmer

Certain titles within some occupational settings are actually gendered terms, for example the nursing rank of 'Sister'. What are male nurses who reach the position of Sister called? Are there other similarly gendered terms – what about the qualifications of 'Bachelor of Arts' and 'Master of Arts'?

You could give your research a good linguistic focus by looking at some job ads and seeing whether job titles appear to suggest a male or female figure as the ideal applicant. This would entail looking not just at obvious terms such as 'waitress/waiter', but also at whether gender is implied in the qualities being asked for – for example, 'bubbly, bright personality', 'stamina', etc.

3   Do a survey of young children's books such as 'ABC' and early reading books to see what category members and cognitive models are portrayed. Pay particular attention to the types of people shown in different social roles, and how they are seen to speak to each other.

4   Research how our common titles – Mr, Ms, Mrs, Miss – are marked and used: What are the origins of these terms? What information do they carry? What are current attitudes towards them and uses of them? Are there differences in spoken and written usage?

U n i t four

Political correctness

Aim of this unit

This unit aims to explore the complex issue called 'political correctness', so that you are better able to analyse what people mean when they use this phrase.

Activity

Brainstorm as many examples of political correctness in language use as you can. If possible, work with a partner or in a group situation, so that you can jog each other's memory about terms that you have heard. When you have finished, have your list beside you to refer to as you work through the material that follows.

Note that there is no commentary on this activity.

Where did the term 'political correctness' come from?

According to Deborah Cameron (1995), the term 'political correctness' was originally used in a disapproving way by left-wing groups in the 1960s and 1970s to refer to their own group members who toed the party line very strictly and whose behaviour was therefore seen as 'ultra-correct'. But, as Cameron points out, the phrase has undergone 'discursive drift', so that it no longer means one thing and one thing only. For example, the term has been used frequently, particularly since the 1980s, by right-wing commentators whose intention has been to criticise aspects of social reform.

What follows is an exploration of some of the recurrent themes underlying discussions of political correctness where *language* is at issue.

Language myths

One aspect of the debate to clear up straightaway is that there have been many examples of so-called 'political correctness' in language use that are completely fictional: in other words, not all the examples of terms you are likely to have come up with have ever been used in real communication contexts. In many cases, terms have been invented in order to criticise those who wanted to make changes. Made-up terms have often involved very exaggerated uses. This is a familiar **rhetorical** technique, for purposes of satire: taking ideas to extremes can be an effective way to ridicule them. Here are some examples of *fictional cases*.

During the 1980s there were reports in the right-wing press that various 'loony left' London councils had done the following:

* banned the word 'manhole' because it was sexist;
* banned the terms 'black coffee', 'blackboard' and 'black bin liners' because they were racist;
* banned the nursery rhyme 'baa baa black sheep' for the same reason.

Cameron points out that, where serious journalists have tried to verify such allegations, they have discovered them to be unfounded. But, she claims, examples such as these take a hold to the extent that people don't question their authenticity. So, in effect, such stories and terms take on a life of their own as we pass them on to each other as anecdotes. Sometimes, there is a story or event that did occur in reality, but the meaning that is taken from it and elaborated in circulation is something quite different. For example, in 2006, the UK press reported a case of racial harassment among workers on the London underground, including an incident in which a white worker bit the head off a black jellybaby (small piece of candy shaped like a baby) in the face of his black colleague. A rumour that did the rounds after that (via emails and face-to-face 'have you heard the latest?' anecdotes) was that black jellybabies were to be banned because of 'political correctness'. At no point in the original story was that idea even remotely suggested.

This process of **intertextual** reshaping and reorientation has been made easier and faster by the advent of new technologies: individuals and news agencies can trade stories at the touch of a button, and an insatiable demand for new items and fast turnover militates against accurate fact-checking. However, all systems leave a trace, and there are now websites that devote themselves to exposing how stories such as the above have come into existence (for example, snopes.com, whose strapline is 'rumor has it'). To see how this works, read the fictional story, reported in both the US and the UK Press, about a worker who supposedly remained dead at his desk, unnoticed, for five days (www.snopes.com/horrors/gruesome/fivedays.asp).

Although the process you have been observing relies on a hi-tech environment for both its original transmission and later exposure, there is a much older but very low-tech tradition of the same thing, in the form of oral storytelling. In face-to-face contexts, we have always told each other stories about supposedly real happenings. On some occasions, though, the events in question turn out to be **urban myths** – in other words, modern fairy stories. One example is shown in Text 4:1. This story is often set on Dartmoor in the UK, but storytellers vary in where the story is supposed to have occurred. For example, a German exchange student we taught insisted it happened in the Black Forest in Germany.

Text 4:1 Urban myth

A man and woman are driving in a car that runs out of petrol. The road is dark and deserted, and the man takes a can and goes to get some petrol, telling his wife to lock the car doors and wait for him. At the time of the story, there is a dangerous, mentally disturbed prisoner on the loose. After a long wait, the woman hears a strange thumping noise on the roof of the car. Then she sees a police car draw up and a loud hailer tells her to come out of the car, go toward the police car and not look back. She gets out and runs away from the car, but, as she does so, she can't help looking back. What she sees when she does so is a deranged man sitting on the roof of her car, playing ball with her husband's severed head.

Activity

Brainstorm any stories you have heard like the one above. Where did you hear the story, and how did the storyteller convince you it was true? Here are the 'abstracts' of some further stories you might have heard:

- the Chinese restaurant where the customer points to his poodle in order to get the dog a drink, but the dog is taken away and cooked for the customer's dinner;

- the young woman who goes to see a male stripper and gets genital crabs in her eye when a pair of his underpants lands on her head.

Now think about the 'politically correct' terms you have on your list. Try to remember where you heard the terms – did the speaker or writer give you any evidence? How do you know the terms really exist? Below are some more mythical examples. Did you have any of these on your list? What about the earlier terms that were supposed to have come from London councils: did any of these feature in your brainstorm and, if so, where did you hear about them originally?

- Having to substitute 'person' for 'man', as in, for example, 'Personchester' instead of 'Manchester', 'personfully' instead of 'manfully', etc.

- Phrases involving the word 'challenged' as in, for example, 'physically challenged' instead of 'disabled', 'vertically challenged' instead of 'short', etc.

Do some more online investigation of the snopes.com site. Here are some stories to follow up:

www.snopes.com/politics/religion/holocaust.asp
www.snopes.com/politics/religion/dollarcoin.asp
www.snopes.com/crime/intent/reply.asp
www.snopes.com/horrors/madmen/mallgrab.asp.

Commentary

You could say that what connects all the different sorts of myths above is the idea of fear. Urban myths are often about modern fears, such as that of psychopathic killers and sexually transmitted diseases. The myth about the Chinese restaurant rehearses the theme of xenophobia via the 'horrifying' nature of foreign eating customs. These modern urban tales are often likened to fairy tales because the latter are also about fears – of abandonment, of death, of the cruelty of the adult world and so on.

But it is not enough to say that urban myths are about fears, for we need to ask whose fears they articulate. In the Chinese restaurant myth, it is the fear experienced by the Westerner that gets expressed. What about the male stripper story? You could see this as acting as a kind of warning to girls against sexual promiscuity, in the same way that the 'Little Red Riding Hood' story warns girls to stay on the straight and narrow.

In the same way, myths about politically correct language embody the fears that particular groups of people feel. They are often expressions of fear by the more powerful groups in society that the status quo might have to change, and not in their favour. So these language myths often derive from right-wing sources, and they satirise ideas about the claims of less powerful groups – women, black people, disabled people. In this case, then, political correctness is all about resisting or denying the claims of such groups to a share in power.

Linguistic neutrality?

The idea that links together all the work you have done so far in this book is that language is not 'neutral'. While it may reflect reality in the sense that it reflects how we have organised society, for the same reason it does not reflect equality, because the different social groups that make up our culture have not been treated equally. So, for many years, groups and individuals who have been working for equality have periodically focused on language in order to change attitudes and raise awareness of discrimination. It's important to stress that language reform has never been seen as an end in itself, but as part of a larger attempt to change the power relationships in society.

Reforming language

Calls for language reforms have been made by many different groups, not just by feminists. Since this is a book on language and gender, analysis of language as it relates to men and women is our central focus. But you will already have noticed that the issue of political correctness and language reform is one that cuts across the representation of a variety of groups.

Groups calling for language reforms in order to work towards more equal opportunities for the sexes have often differed in their strategies and in the degree of reform they have thought necessary. The material that follows aims to give you an understanding of the two main traditions within this area. Both of these traditions have produced examples of new language items that some commentators might label as 'politically correct'.

The liberal tradition

A very moderate, liberal approach can be seen in the work of Casey Miller and Kate Swift, who wrote *The Handbook of Non-Sexist Writing* (1981), a book that has acted as a guide for serious journalists for many years. The rationale for this liberal tradition is that it is possible for language to be made more representative of different groups and, in order to bring about fairer representation, language practices need to be changed in various ways. This sometimes mean inventing new terms where old ones will not do.

Below, in italics, are the main areas put forward as needing attention. In some cases, you will be referred back to Unit three, as some aspects mentioned below have already been covered there.

See whether any of the suggestions for new job titles (no. 3, below) occurred in your original brainstorm on 'political correctness'. The difference between these examples and the phrases previously called 'language myths' is that the job titles below were intended for real use and have in many cases been used in public and official contexts.

1   *The use of 'man' as a false generic* (see Unit three).

2   *The pronoun problem* (see Unit three).

3   *Discriminatory job titles.* Examples (with alternatives) are taken from the US Dept of Labor *Job Title Revisions* (3rd edition, 1975). Note that the revisions were trying to combat ageism as well as sexism:

Original term	*New term*
airline steward, stewardess	flight attendant
foreman	supervisor
salesman	salesperson
seamstress	sewer

signalman	signaller
watchman	guard
draftsman	drafter
junior executive	executive trainee
cameraman	camera operator
office girl, boy	office helper
repairman	repairer
fireman	firefighter
spokesman	spokesperson
policeman	police officer
chairman	chairperson, the chair
housewife	house manager

4   *Generalisations.* This is where, although no specific sex-reference is present, writers obviously have a specific group in mind, and are generalising from that group to everyone. Examples:

- 'The average person finds it no problem at all to have three headcolds, one sunburn, an attack of athlete's foot, 20 headaches, three hangovers and five temper tantrums with adolescent children, and still get in his 61 hours of shaving.'

- 'H.G. Wells has the ability to exert his magnetism on the small boy in all of us.'

- 'Sharing our railway compartment were two Norwegians and their wives.'

5   *Non-parallel treatment.* Miller and Swift divide this aspect into several areas, as below. Limitations of space prevent a long list of examples, but you should be familiar with these ideas as a result of the work you did on newspapers in Unit two:

- describing women by appearance, but men by achievement;

- describing women by their relationship to men, but not describing men by their relationship to women;

- referring to women as 'girls' but giving male figures the adult label, 'men';

- often using fixed collocations where the male referents occur first – as in 'he or she', 'husband and wife', 'men and women'.

Miller and Swift were advocating some practical reforms that consisted of trying to encourage communicators to think about the possible effects of their language uses. To this extent, they were aiming to make representations of men and women fairer and more equal. But the notion that language could – or even should – be made to represent men and women equally is not an idea that has gained universal acceptance.

The radical tradition

A feminist tradition very different from that represented by Miller and Swift has rejected the idea that language can be 'improved' by making small adjustments such as those proposed above. This more radical tradition has maintained that women have been forced to use a language that is not their own and that they therefore cannot use to express their experiences effectively: in other words, they have been forced to see the world through male eyes. This is because women have been excluded historically from the production of powerful public discourses. Smith (1978) describes this process:

> This is how a tradition is formed. A way of thinking develops in this discourse through the medium of the printed word as well as in speech. It has questions, solutions, themes, styles, standards, ways of looking at the world. These are formed as the circle of those present builds on the work of the past. From these circles women have been excluded . . . they have never controlled the material or social means to the making of a tradition among themselves or to acting as equals in the ongoing discourse of intellectuals.

Activity

What is meant by 'ways of looking at the world' (in the quotation above) could easily take another whole book to explore. But here are some examples for you to think about, discuss and research. You could start this process by doing some investigations of vocabulary in any dictionaries, etymologies and textbooks you have to hand. The examples below are all from academics in different subject areas researching ideas about sexual experiences, and many are quoted in Spender (1980). They are all claiming that our language as it exists at present gives men and women very different stories about sexual behaviour and about the importance of their sexual experiences. How far do you think their ideas are valid?

- There is no term for normal sexual power in women, to match the term 'virile' or 'potent' for men. There are only the extremes of 'frigid' and 'nymphomaniac'.

- Terms for sexual intercourse – such as 'penetration' – are invariably male-oriented; if women had named the same thing, the English language might have the term 'enclosure' instead.

- Why is the term 'rape' not considered taboo, while another four-letter word describing female genitals is often considered the strongest taboo word in the English language?

- There are large discrepancies between the numbers and types of terms available to label women as promiscuous – such as 'tart' and 'slag' – and those available to label men. Terms for women are not only more numerous but also more derogatory than those for men, for whom promiscuity can be associated with prowess.

- Many medical textbooks link female genitals with reproduction (i.e. focus on ovaries and womb rather than clitoris), but male genitals with sexual intercourse and pleasure. For example, Dorling Kindersley's *Children's Dictionary* (on CD-ROM, 1996) has the following for male and female genitals:

    penis: the part of a man's body that he uses to urinate or to have sex;

    vagina: the passage that connects the outside of a woman's body to her womb;

    clitoris: no reference.

- While female sexuality is either described in negative ways or not described at all, male sexuality is at the basis of some very positive and high-status words. For example, the words 'seminal', 'seminar' and 'disseminate' have the same derivation as that of the term 'semen'.

Note that there is no commentary on this activity.

The terms above are all examples of what the poet Adrienne Rich has called 'telling it slant' (1979, p. 208) – the way in which many women, according to some radical feminist critics, have had to define their experiences in spite of the available language, and not through it. For such critics, changing language in the way that Miller and Swift advocate is pointless, because it's just tinkering at the edges. A radical view would see the whole language system as **phallocratic** and **patriarchal**, and would say that we needed to unpick all our social discourses to reveal the thinking that lies behind them. This view doesn't seek to patch up an imperfect language system, but to challenge and disrupt uses of language that are not normally seen as problematic, in order to show up our social power lines.

Text 4:2 Radical writers

Writer 1

Suzette Hayden Elgin, an anthropologist as well as a novelist, invented a new language called 'Laadan' in her *Mother Tongue* novels. Elgin uses new lexical items to encode what she sees as common female experiences. Here are some examples (Elgin, 1981):

acanthophile: A woman who repeatedly chooses to form relationships with persons who abuse or neglect her, despite apparent unhappiness each time. (From Gr. 'acanthos', 'thorn'.)

bordweal: An artificial barrier raised to keep women out of things, such as an irrelevant height requirement. (From O.E. 'bord-weal', 'a wall of shields'.)

to granny: To apply the wisdom and the experience of the elderly woman to any situation.

scratscrak: A night spent tending children, the sick, the helpless, while male members of the household sleep peacefully through it all; an ugly word coined to be ugly. You'll have no trouble pronouncing it.

Writer 2

Mary Daly, a feminist theologian, wrote (with Jane Caputi) an 'alternative' dictionary, *The Websters First New Inter galactic Wickedary* (1987). Here are two entries from it:

Spinster *n*: a woman whose occupation is to Spin, to participate in the whirling movement of creation; one who has chosen her Self, who defines her Self by choice neither in relation to children nor to men; one who is Self-identified; a whirling dervish, Spiraling in New Time/Space.

Old Maid *n*: a Crone who has steadfastly resisted imprisonment in the Comatose State of matrimony.

Text 4:2 shows two examples of radical writers whose aim is to challenge our thinking by inventing new terms or by giving existing ones new meanings. It's important to realise that these writers are engaged in a very different task from Miller and Swift. For a start, these radical writers are not suggesting that the terms they invent should be part of our everyday language use: their aim is to raise our consciousness rather than help us write an everyday text. Also, both writers are working with creative licence to create types of narrative whose purpose is to propose alternative 'realities'. To this extent, they are closer to writers of fiction such as George Orwell, who invented new types of language in *1984*, or to Anthony Burgess, who did the same in *A Clockwork Orange*.

The 'wickedary' is a playful exercise, but it has a serious purpose – to raise awareness of how dictionary makers have acted as 'authorities' in traditionally defining the sexes, and particularly the female sex, in very restricted and potentially damaging ways. Webster's is a very well-known and longstanding American dictionary; Daly's Websters' diction-ary spins several webs of new associations, inventing new terms and reclaiming many old ones, particularly those that have traditionally been used negatively to refer to women, such as 'crone', 'battle-axe', 'hag', 'nag', 'gossip' and 'witch'. She also divides existing words up in a new way and gives them a new morphological structure. Here are some examples, illustrating all these strategies:

Crone-logical *adj*: be-ing in accordance with the clarifying logic of Crones; able to see through man's mysteries/misteries; marked by a refusal to be side-tracked by the tedious, tidy, tiny, and ill-logical steps of male methodology/methodolatry.

olds, the: the same old stories: patriarchal 'news' as reported/distorted by the assorted officious olds agencies and disseminated in the daily oldspapers.

phallosophy *n*: inflated foolosophy: 'wisdom' loaded with seminal ideas and disseminated by means of thrusting arguments.

Syn-Crone-icities *n*: 'coincidences' experienced and recognised by Crones as Strangely significant.

the/rapist *n*: a psycho-ologist who practises what he preaches/teaches.

It is unlikely that you will have had any of the terms from the radical tradition on your original list of 'politically correct' items. But you may have done because, when books such as those above have been reviewed, items of language have sometimes been picked out and ridiculed by right-wing commentators who have pretended to believe that the writers were advocating the use of these terms in everyday discourse.

The language is under attack!

Objectors to language reform often lump together all the different sorts of language examples we have looked at, and call them examples of 'politically correct' language.

The suggestion is typically that the language is adhering to a political line that either favours disadvantaged groups, or that does them a disservice by inventing new terms instead of campaigning for equality in more effective and practical ways. In the process, the language system itself is often characterised as being under attack and in need of protection from new and dangerous forms of 'thought police'. These ideas will be considered one by one in this final section.

The thought police are coming

The idea of 'interfering' with language is an interesting one, because it assumes that language is naturally occurring rather than humanly constructed. It is easy to feel as though the origins of language were far in the past, and that the process of meaning creation is over and done with. Yet this process is going on all the time, under our noses. Following is one example, taken from Spender (1980).

An experiment was conducted to compare male and female visual perception, where subjects were asked to look at a picture and could either separate the stimulus (an embedded figure) from the background or else see the stimulus and background as a whole picture. It was found that men were more likely to do the former, and women the latter.

The scientists conducting the experiment called the male behaviour 'field independence', and the female behaviour 'field dependence'. Spender asks what the difference in connotations would have been if the male behaviour had been described as 'context blindness' and the female behaviour 'context awareness'. Spender's terms would have fitted the experimental results just as well, but the connotations of male and female behaviour would have been very different.

Cameron (1995) suggests that the strength of objections to language changes may be associated with the fact that the objector is being forced to see his or her own language use as not universally accepted – that others have a different understanding of terms. This means that there is no 'safe' place – whether you say, 'chairman', 'madam chairman', 'chairperson' or 'chair' says something about you. 'Politically correct' language causes anxiety because it is 'a challenge to the whole idea of a universal and neutral language' (Cameron, 1995, p. 120).

Just what are you supposed to call them these days?

One frequent aspect of complaints about 'politically correct' language is that the terms that are acceptable are constantly changing. For example, should you say 'homosexual' or 'gay'? Is black still OK, or should it be 'people of colour'? Should it be 'mixed race' or 'bi-racial'? Are people in wheelchairs 'disabled' or 'wheelchair users'? Are older people 'elderly', 'elder adults' or 'senior citizens'? Are children with learning problems 'slow learners' or 'children with special needs'?

If you stand back from these terms, you will notice that there are hidden categories above, categories that are not mentioned in all this labelling. Those are the categories that represent the norm in each case: heterosexual, white, pure (as opposed to 'mixed'), mono-racial, able-bodied, young, normal learners.

An important point to note, then, is that the process of labelling is one of identifying difference from a norm and that objectors to change often belong to that invisible and unstated norm from which others are judged as deviant. This idea of categorisation and norm construction was at the core of the work you did in Unit three. While those labelled are constantly being relabelled because their new labels attract negative meanings, people who represent the 'norm' are never labelled at all – they are just 'people'.

Another important aspect to note is that changes in terms are not arbitrary or whimsical, but happen for good reasons. For example, consider these labels, which were attached to the groups above in previous years (in some cases, until quite recently):

queer

nigger

half-caste

half-breed

cripple

old age pensioner

mentally retarded.

More recent changes – say, from 'black American' to 'African American' – also signify important shifts in perspective. This particular change alters the label from one of physical appearance and skin colour to ideas about heritage and culture. Consider the uproar that would ensue if someone suggested that Italians, Spanish and British people should all be lumped together under the label 'whites'. Consider the fuss at present about even being called 'European'.

Sometimes, labels are rejected or thought of negatively because of the history of their invention and because of who has 'owned' the term. For example, the term 'homosexual' came from the days when the medical profession saw being gay as a pathological illness, whereas 'gay' is a term invented by gay people themselves.

Naming and reclaiming

Cameron suggests that the whole phenomenon of language reform challenges the majority power group's assumptions that they can define the world: 'At stake is a power structure in which certain people, often without being conscious of it, just assume the right to tell other people who they are' (1995, p. 144).

Changes in naming can also represent a group's reaction to its own label; to being given an identity by others. This can mean that, sometimes, a group will defiantly use a label that has been given as a negative representation, and turn that label into something positive. You saw this process in Mary Daly's use of the term 'crone'.

The reclaiming of terms can be seen as a form of group resistance, but it gives objectors to language reform further grounds for complaint: why should Daly and her colleagues be able to use the term 'crone' to each other, thereby appearing rather 'politically incorrect', when men have been told for years that this is an insulting term that is off-limits?

Political correctness and context

The reclaiming of terms by groups who have been traditionally labelled in negative ways undoubtedly makes life more difficult for those in majority power groups who have not been on the receiving end of such labels. That is partly the point of the exercise. So, while women can address each other affectionately as 'girls', while gay men and women have developed new forms of analysis called 'Queer Theory', and while young black men might use 'nigger' to each other as a positive form of address, the use of these terms to or about these groups by people who are outsiders produces a very different set of connotations. Who is talking and to whom, plus all the other contextual factors of language use, make up what we call the 'meaning' of any term.

Group resistance to forms of negative labelling has arguably forced everyone to do more thinking about the language they use. If the tradition of complaint about 'political correctness' has arisen because of the discomfiture of majority power groups, this looks like a very positive development. It is positive because it means that those in powerful positions will have to pay more attention to those who are less privileged.

Summary

In breaking down what is meant by the term 'political correctness', three different types of language use were identified as commonly being labelled under this heading:

- new language items that are mythical, devised for purposes of satire by right-wing commentators;
- new language items that have been suggested by liberal critics, for use in real contexts;
- new language items that have been created by radical critics, in order to reveal prevalent ideologies, but not necessarily for everyday use.

It was suggested that the term 'political correctness' itself was typically used by people who object to language reform per se, and who would classify all the examples above as wrongful and misguided uses of English.

This unit went on to look at particular aspects of the 'political correctness' debate:

- the idea of the language system as under attack by new controlling forces;
- the idea of the rapid changes in terms;
- the idea of resistance and disruption.

Extension activities

1   Do a survey in order to discover what people understand by the term 'political correctness'. You could use some of the different examples of terms quoted in this unit, and get them to classify terms they think are acceptable or not.

2   Look up the term 'political correctness' in a newly published dictionary to see if it is defined and, if so, how. Collect any examples of articles about this issue in newspapers – for example, from the letters pages.

3   Review Miller and Swift's areas of language use that need attention. Focus on one or two areas and research current usage in texts of your choice.

4   Research language use about sexual experiences. For example, you could look at advice books aimed at teenagers, or pamphlets on sex education, or at problem pages in magazines. You could also investigate medical textbooks, contemporary and old.

5   Make up some new terms for experiences that you don't think get encoded. Here are some ideas: always being the one who has to go to the counter to order food/drink; being flattered into doing menial jobs such as washing up or ironing because 'you do them so well', etc.

6   Investigate some internet sites, such as snopes.com and language monitor.com, which collect and analyse media stories and their associated language use. Critically evaluate the examples you find there – remember that every site has its own ideology.

Gender and speech styles

Introduction

We appear to have many ideas about how men and women use language and, in particular, how they *differ* in their language use. One very general question to ask straightaway is why we are so interested in difference rather than similarity. This is not an easy question to answer, but it is something that you need to have in the back of your mind throughout this unit. It has probably occurred to you already, during your work in earlier units, but the quest for 'difference' seems to loom particularly large when male and female speech styles are under consideration. For example, here are the titles of two of the most commercially successful books of the 1990s about male and female communication and language:

Men are from Mars, Women are from Venus
You Just Don't Understand: Men and women in conversation

Do you think the following invented titles could have been best-sellers too?:

Women and Men are Both from Jupiter
I Know Just What You Mean: Women and men in conversation

Difference is big news in the popular press and in magazines, too. You only have to look as far as the latest feature in *GQ* or *Cosmopolitan* on how to interpret the language of your partner, to find male and female 'versions' of language treated as though they were mutually unintelligible foreign languages. Are they really, or does treating them in this way make for good media copy?

Aim of this unit

The aim of this unit is to help you explore the whole idea of male and female 'difference' in language use. In order to do this, you will need to take in something of the history of research on gender and speech styles, because there has been a considerable amount of research done, and because academic ideas have changed significantly over the years. Also, the academic world, however much we might like to think otherwise, is part of society and, as such, is itself subject to gender stereotyping. Because of the need to cover a lot of ground, you will find that the style in this unit is less interactive than that of the other units in this book. But it is hoped that, as a result of working through the unit, you will have an increased awareness of the thinking that you yourself bring to any research that you do, as well as an ability to be more critical of the research findings of others.

Folklinguistics

How a Lady Should Behave Out of Doors

In her behaviour out of doors, the gentlewoman is quiet and unassuming. She shuns any exaggeration of dress and fashion that would make her conspicuous; it is not her aim to attract the eye of the crowd, but to escape its notice. She does not sweep the pavement with trailing skirts or address her friends in loud tones. Neither does she attract attention by her boisterous laughter. The aim of the gentlewoman is to escape notice out of doors; that of the ill-bred woman to attract it. Therein lies the difference.

(Jack and Strauss, *The Woman's Book: Contains everything a woman ought to know*, 1911, p. 327)

The first thing to explore is the extent to which we have embedded concepts in our culture about the way men and women speak, or the way they *should* speak. Because language is a form of behaviour, ideas about

82

the language that is appropriate for men and women often find expression in books of social etiquette, such as the above. Actually, that's not quite true. It would be more accurate to say that social etiquette books have always dealt more with female behaviour, as male behaviour has traditionally been seen as the norm and in need of no particular advice or attention.

As well as the prescriptions and proscriptions of advice books, we also have popular sayings about male and female language, such as 'nice girls don't swear' and 'swearing like a trooper'. In these examples, the nature of the language remains unspecified because we rely on shared linguistic and cultural knowledge to fill in the gaps. For example, we know that the type of swearing the trooper (foot-soldier, male by default) is going in for is not going to be along the lines of 'oh dear' or 'oh bother'; equally, we know that 'nice girls don't swear' really means 'nice girls don't use four-letter words' and that the word 'nice' refers to public reputation – girls who are rated as respectable – rather than individual personality.

But even where we don't have expressions referring specifically to the language of women and men, you don't have to work very hard to pull up a host of associations about talk and gender. And here, too, we are dealing with hidden assumptions about male and female linguistic behaviour. For example, if someone said a woman was 'talking like a lady' or 'talking in a ladylike way', what might the speaker be implying? How might that differ from 'talking like a woman', or even 'talking like an old woman'? What about 'she's got a mouth like a fishwife'? What might someone mean if they referred to 'man talk', 'guy talk', 'bloke-ish talk', or 'laddish talk'?; and how about 'women's talk' or 'girl talk'? In Unit two, we focused particularly on the connotations of words, and Unit three explored ideas about norms and stereotyping. Here we are looking at the stereotypical connections we make between speech styles and gender (plus other social dimensions – for example, ideas about social class and age are clearly at work in many of the expressions quoted so far).

When beliefs are encoded in language in the form of popular sayings, this is often called **folklinguistics** – popular beliefs about language. The idea is that such sayings are a bit like proverbs in being part of the cultural luggage we inherit from our community as we acquire language. The term 'folklinguistics' sounds rather quaint, conjuring up ideas of rustic life and folk dancing. But, as you'll see, popular beliefs about language are certainly not harmless.

Note: Several activities follow, after which there is an overall commentary.

Activity

Explore the possible connections between the folklinguistic expression 'nice girls don't swear' and the newspaper article in Text 5:1. The article itself is confusing in its description of events, but what do you make of the way the crime is reported, particularly in the wording of the headline?

Text 5:1 Woman's words

> ### WOMAN'S WORDS 'TOO MUCH' FOR SOLDIERS
>
> The language of a woman soldier said to have been raped by a gang of paratroopers was too much for at least two other men, Winchester Crown Court was told yesterday.
>
> The two soldiers gave evidence in the trial at which 13 members of the Parachute Regiment deny raping or indecently assaulting a woman soldier, aged 23, in the paratroops barracks at Bulford camp, Wiltshire, last November.
>
> One said he was awoken from his sleep by shouting and a woman's scream. He looked out of his door, saw a bare-legged woman and some soldiers in a corridor. 'I thought trouble was coming so I left,' he said.
>
> The case continues.
>
> (*The Guardian*, 1990)

Activity

Think about and discuss the expressions referred to on the two previous pages. The expressions are a mixture of well-known sayings (such as 'nice girls don't swear') and hypothetical utterances (such as 'talking in a ladylike way'). Regardless of how common the expression is, this activity centres on the same question: what might each expression reveal about our culturally embedded ideas on gender and talk? Here are the expressions again:

Swearing like a trooper

Nice girls don't swear

Talking in a ladylike way

Talking like a woman

Talking like an old woman

She's got a mouth like a fishwife

Men's talk

Bloke-ish talk

Laddish talk

Women's talk

Girl talk

It might be helpful to work through this activity in two stages, first thinking about the language itself, then about the supposed speakers.

The language

What kind of talk is being suggested in each case? For example, is the focus on:

- vocabulary items?
- the topics covered in the talk?
- the way the talk is managed by the participants?
- accent?

The speakers

How are men and women being represented? For example, is the focus on their:

- social class?
- age?
- sexual behaviour or sexuality?
- conformity to an ideal of masculinity/femininity?

Taking expressions such as the above out of context can be a starting point for thinking about our cultural values, but meaning can only be fully determined in context – in other words, by thinking about who is speaking, and where, and for what purpose. With this idea in mind, to what extent might the meaning of the expressions you have been studying be changed by who is saying them, and in what context?

Finally, add any further items that you think reveal our ideas about male and female language styles. You might also play around with the expressions above and see what effects are produced by making them refer to the opposite sex.

Here are some examples:

> Swearing like a nursery nurse
> Nice boys don't swear
> Boy talk
> Talking like a gentleman
> He's got a mouth like a fishhusband
> Talking like a man
> Talking like an old man

Activity

Read the poem by Liz Lochhead (Text 5:2). What is this poem saying about male and female speech styles?

Text 5:2 Men Talk (Rap)

Men Talk (Rap)

Women
Rabbit rabbit rabbit women
Tattle and titter
Women prattle
Women waffle and witter

Men Talk. Men Talk.

Women into Girl Talk
About Women's Trouble
Trivia 'n' Small Talk
They yap and they babble

Men Talk. Men Talk.

Women gossip Women giggle
Women niggle-niggle-niggle
Men Talk.

Women yatter
Women chatter
Women chew the fat, women spill the beans
Women ain't been takin'
The oh-so Good Advice in them
Women's Magazines.

A Man Likes A Good Listener.
Oh yeah
I like A Woman
Who likes me enough
Not to nitpick
Not to nag and
Not to interrupt cause I call that treason
A woman with the Good Grace
To be struck dumb
By me Sweet Reason. Yes –

A Man Likes a Good Listener
A real
Man
Likes a Real Good Listener
Women yap yap yap
Verbal Diarrhoea is a Female Disease
Woman she spread she rumours round she
Like Philadelphia Cream Cheese.

Oh
Bossy Women Gossip
Girlish Women Giggle
Women natter, women nag
Women niggle niggle niggle

Men Talk.
Men
Think First, Speak Later Men Talk.

(Liz Lochhead, *Dreaming Frankenstein,* 1986)

Commentary

This commentary has been divided into sections, for increased readability.

Gender and social class

A common thread running through some of the data you have been studying is a connection between gender and social class. Both the terms 'lady' and 'gentleman' suggest privileged figures concerned with social etiquette and respectability within 'polite' society. The implication in the phrases 'talking like a lady/gentleman' compared with 'talking like a man/ woman' is that, regardless of gender, people lower down the social scale have 'worse' linguistic habits that their social 'betters'. It is no accident that it's the trooper who is seen as swearing profusely, rather than the brigadier or general, and the fishwife rather than the aristocratic lady.

However, 'lady' and 'gentleman' have had differing histories in terms of their connotations. While both terms still exist in the fixed phrase 'ladies and gentlemen', and as labels on toilet doors, the term 'lady', rather than 'woman', is often used as the equivalent of 'man', while 'gentleman' seems to be restricted in its usage. So, for example, children not looking where they are going will be told 'mind that lady', rather than 'mind that woman'. Feminist analysis has long explained this variation as the result of the way the term 'woman' has acquired negative connotations, so that 'lady' is seen as a 'polite' alternative. For many women, though, 'lady' is something of a false compliment, in having connotations of decorative ornamentation – an ineffectual figure not to be taken seriously, particularly in the workplace. So speaking in a 'ladylike' way may have similar connotations, of polite but trivial talk. Would this kind of talk (and talker) seem appropriate in a business negotiation?

Gender and sexuality

Gender cuts across social class stereotypes in further significant ways, affecting women differently from men. In depictions of women, social class is often linked with sexual behaviour: in the text from the etiquette book, it is only the 'ill-bred' woman who 'attracts the eye of the crowd' by laughing and calling out. A 'lady' should be quiet and inconspicuous, not drawing attention to herself. 'Nice girls don't swear' tells us that, if girls swear, they might forfeit their good reputations: 'nice' in this phrase is not about being friendly or helpful, it is about being sexually chaste and therefore of a good 'class' of woman. The word 'nice' here is sexualised. So, if a woman swears – a very direct way of drawing attention to herself – she is not respectable, not a 'lady'. The *Guardian* article can be read in this way, too. The way the article is written (which is, presumably, a reflection of the way the defence case was presented in court) makes it unclear which was the crime: rape or a woman's language use?

Somehow it seems that a link is being made between the alleged rape and the woman's 'unacceptable' language – such bad language that even paratroopers found it 'too much'. One reading of this is that, because of her 'bad' language, she was not a 'nice' girl (i.e. she was a 'bad' girl) and therefore was not considered worthy of help from the 'two other men' who were not part of the alleged gang-rape. The implication from that is that she deserved what was happening to her. But, even if you don't agree with this reading, there still needs to be some explanation of what relevance a woman's language use can possibly have to her being subjected to an alleged sexual attack.

But it is not simply the case that, while female behaviour is often constructed and interpreted in particular ways, men have freedom to define themselves in any way they want. There are both overt and covert messages about male linguistic behaviour, too; for example, that 'real men' (like troopers) swear a lot and use extreme words. In the reversed phrase, 'nice boys don't swear', 'nice boys' is an unusual collocation, showing us that the norm for masculinity (and therefore 'masculine' language) is 'not nice' – rough, tough, nasty, the stereotype of heterosexual maleness. In looking at types of talk, too, there are different ideas about the nature of men. For example, would 'bloke-ish' or 'laddish' talk encompass the idea of gay men as participants?

Gender and age
Male and female speakers seem to be characterised differently where age is concerned. At first sight, it looks as though an age range is being described, with 'girl talk', 'women's talk' and talking like an 'old woman'. But the age references are deceptive. For a start, 'old woman' is a term that is often used about men rather than women, with the suggestion of fussy behaviour, and on the principle that accusations of 'femaleness' are the ultimate insult to men – the same principle behind terms such as 'sissy'. And references to 'girl' do not necessarily mean 'young woman', since adult women can often be referred to as 'girls'. Spender (1980) suggests that, if you look at the way terms are applied to women, you may be under the impression that women never grow up, since they remain girls until they become 'old girls'.

Gender and ideology
Although we have ideas about the way the sexes talk encoded in our culture, that doesn't mean that words and phrases remain absolutely static or fixed in their meaning, regardless of who is saying them. For example, 'talking like

a woman' could be intended to mean something very positive if used by a feminist speaker, while meaning something very negative if used by an anti-feminist. 'Talking like a man' would not necessarily be a compliment if the speaker had a misandrist (anti-male) view. But the fact remains that, while people have some room to manoeuvre and can reconstruct meanings consciously within their daily discourse, there are meanings that prevail in the wider culture through their constant circulation in particular and powerful domains. So, for example, 'talking like a man' is still likely to imply something a lot more positive and powerful than 'talking like a woman' in our culture's public discourses (McConnell-Ginet, 1998).

Gender and representation

If the explanation above seems to you to suggest that we can hold two very different and somewhat contradictory ideas in our heads at once, then your reading is right. We might ourselves have had experiences that lead us to a particular view, but that might be completely at odds with ideas that are in circulation in the wider culture. As individuals, we 'know' both. A concrete example is the stereotyping of occupations in 'swearing like a trooper/nursery nurse'. We may have met some rather foul-mouthed nursery nurses, and some very well-mannered troopers, but we will still know the traditional stereotypes of these figures. In the same way, the fact that we know men who gossip and nag, or women who are very forthright and assertive in conversation, doesn't stop us from understanding the traditional stereotypes of male and female talk as the reverse of this pattern.

Liz Lochhead's poem adds a further dimension, and that is that the same behaviour by men and women can be labelled differently – men 'talk', while women 'gossip' and 'nag'. In talking about her poem on a BBC video (*The Language File: Nice girls don't swear*), Lochhead explains that her take on this issue was ironic – she is not saying that this is what happens, she is saying that this is how society differentiates in a sexist way. However, she goes on to say that the poem has met with mixed responses when she has performed it in schools and colleges to students. On the one hand, some male listeners have not understood that she was being ironic, thinking she was simply describing 'reality'; on the other hand, some female listeners have said that they see the ways of talk attributed to women as a wide repertoire of talk styles that they were proud of, and that they rated their talk skills more highly than those of male speakers who have only one way of expressing them-selves. This has connections with the idea of language reclamation that you studied in Unit four.

A history of research on gender and speech styles

There are comments about male and female language in our cultural written archives as far back as the Bible, but one of the first linguists to give the area the stamp of academic authority in modern times was Otto Jesperson, in his *Language: Its nature, development and origin* (1922), which was a very influential and highly rated book for many years. His chapter on sex differences in language speaks volumes by its title: 'The woman'. In other words, men are seen as the norm and women as departing from that norm in various ways – as being deviant. Jesperson pays most attention to vocabulary differences and, despite having only anecdotal evidence for what he says, gives a long list of male and female lexical variations. However, more interesting than the actual examples are the generalised judgements that he makes about what these variations amount to. For example, women are seen as having limited vocabularies: 'the vocabulary of a woman as a rule is much less extensive than that of a man . . .'. They are also described as being rather delicate, easily offended and oblique:

> There can be no doubt that women exercise a great and universal influence on linguistic development through their instinctive shrinking from coarse and gross expressions and their preference for refined, and (in certain spheres) veiled and indirect expressions.

Jesperson claims that men are the people who invent new terms, while women are innately conservative: 'men are the chief renovators of language . . .'. He also sees women as having a dulling effect on language use:

> Men will certainly with great justice object that there is a danger of the language becoming languid and insipid if we are always to content ourselves with women's expressions and that vigour and vividness count for something.

Early feminist critiques of language pointed to writers such as Jesperson, and to earlier figures such as prescriptive eighteenth-century grammarians, in order to show how stereotyped ideas about women's language have been written into academic discourses as **received opinion**. One such critique was Robin Lakoff's *Language and Woman's Place* (1975).

Lakoff's central point was that women were socialised into sounding like 'ladies', which then in turn kept them in their place because being 'ladylike' is a bar to being 'powerful' in our culture. This is because power is associated with male behaviour and male discourse. In other words, women were being trained to sound inferior. At the time, the idea of women being in a no-win situation – if they talked like 'ladies' they were seen as powerless and trivial, but if they talked like men they were seen as unfeminine – struck a chord with many people, including feminist researchers. But two aspects of this kind of approach led to some unfortunate results, which are outlined below.

First, the idea above often ended up being interpreted as meaning that there was something wrong with the way women used language, so it was women who needed to change their behaviour if they wanted access to power. Associated with this was the idea that, if their 'language problem' was sorted out, then women would be given fairer treatment and would somehow be more successful. This is not necessarily what Robin Lakoff was herself saying in any direct way – remember that there is often a gulf between the complexity of research findings and how those findings are distilled in the wider culture. While research itself is often very revealing about the thinking of the researcher, the way research is summarised and reported is just as revealing about the values of the culture in and beyond the academic world.

The idea that there might be something intrinsically wrong with the language of a disadvantaged group (as opposed to something wrong with our attitudes towards them) is now called the **deficit model** of language. This term has been coined with the benefit of hindsight, but it is a mistake to view such thinking as exclusively a thing of the past.

Activity

Discuss how the language of the following groups is thought about and described now in our culture. Is there any evidence that a deficit model of their language exists?

- People with regional accents.
- Speakers using non-standard grammar (e.g. we was, I were, they ain't, I never done it).
- Writers using non-standard grammar.
- Speakers of Afro-Caribbean Patwa.

Note that there is no commentary on this activity.

The idea of a deficit model of women's language has led to an array of courses designed for women to become more 'effective': for example, assertiveness-training or management-training courses for women, teaching them how to sound more authoritative and be taken more seriously. In short, an industry of language remediation has been making a good living out of the deficit idea. This also applies, of course, to other groups' so-called language deficiencies: think of speech-training courses where the norm is **received pronunciation** (**RP**), or literacy programmes that are sets of drills for Standard English. But a further aspect of language deficit work has arisen out of early books such as Robin Lakoff's (see above), and that is work that has been very much within linguistic research itself. You might call this work 'deficit feature-spotting' because it has consisted of chasing small items of language that were seen by Lakoff as characterising female usage. Some examples are given below.

1   The use of terms relating to traditionally female work (such as working with fabrics) – for example, a greater range of terms for colours than men use (e.g. aquamarine, fuchsia, lavender, etc., instead of more basic terms such as blue or red).
2   'Empty' adjectives such as 'charming', 'cute' (American English usage).
3   Intensifiers such as 'so', in phrases such as 'that's so good'.
4   The use of tag questions – where a statement is turned into a question by putting a tag on the end, as in 'the meeting is at eight o'clock, isn't it?'
5   Use of 'hedges' such as 'kind of and 'you know'.

Nowadays, the idea of researching small items such as the above in terms of male and female usage is seen as rather dubious, for a number of reasons.

The 'so what?' criticism

So what if men and women use some aspects of language differently, particularly vocabulary? Wouldn't that be what you'd expect if men and women were told from an early age that they should be interested in different areas? What is often more interesting than the supposed differences themselves are the conclusions that are drawn from such findings. For example, Jesperson quotes research where 25 university students were asked to write down 100 words as quickly as possible. It was found that many of the men's words related to the animal kingdom, while many of the women's words related to fabrics and food. The conclusions from this were that:

> In general the feminine traits are an attention to the immediate surroundings, to the finished product, to the ornamental, the individual, and the concrete; while the masculine preference is for the more remote, the constructive, the useful, the general and the abstract.
>
> (Ellis, 1904, p. 189)

While it takes something of an imaginative leap to get from the original examples to the summary, it seems bizarre that knowing the names of animals was seen as more 'constructive and useful' than knowing about fabrics and food!

The linguistic relativity criticism

Itemising language in this way suggests that a language feature has only one possible meaning and that the meaning is somehow contained in the structure. So, for example, Lakoff suggests that tag questions are signals of uncertainty, because they ask for reassurance. But what about the following phrases: are these expressions of uncertainty, just because they are tag questions?

Nice day, isn't it?

You won't do *that* again, *will* you?

You're a nasty bit of work, aren't you?

Tag questions are complex items that can convey a range of different meanings where much depends on how they are said and the relationship between the interlocutors. In fact, shortly after the publication of Lakoff's book, two researchers (Dubois and Crouch, 1975) researched the use of tag questions in an academic setting and found that men used them more. Interestingly, the idea that men were therefore hesitant and lacking confidence didn't catch on.

The language context criticism

Language usage and how it is viewed are powerfully affected by context, including the setting and purpose of the interaction. Basing their work on Lakoff's idea that some aspects of women's language signal hesitancy, two researchers (O'Barr and Atkins, 1980) examined the use of hedging features (for example, 'sort of', 'kind of') in a courtroom setting, and found that people judged speakers who used such features as less convincing than those who didn't. The researchers concluded that there were certain linguistic features that marked someone's language as 'powerless' in some universal way. The problem was that they didn't take account of the fact that a courtroom setting demands certain kinds of language and if you pepper your utterances in that context with 'sort ofs' then you are bound to be seen as uncertain, whereas in another setting you might not be seen in this way at all.

Linguistic developments

We now know considerably more about the way in which many aspects of spoken language work. As a result, some of the features previously considered 'empty' and redundant – such as 'sort of' – are now seen as fulfilling very important functions. For example, many features of so-called 'vague language', such as '*a bit of* lunch', 'twenty *or so*', 'shopping *and stuff*' or '*about* forty', are understood as crucial aspects of interpersonal communication for everyone, allowing speakers to sound relaxed and informal (Channell, 1994).

The cultural diversity criticism

Much early feminist research was dominated by a white, middle-class, heterosexual, American point of view. In treating women as if they were all in one category, all sorts of other differences were made to disappear, making the research focus very narrow and the explanations of variation even narrower. For example, what kind of woman might use a very elaborate system of colour reference? A fashion designer or interior designer? How many working-class black women become interior designers?

From deficit to dominance: men behaving badly

Two influential later publications – Thorne and Henley's *Language and Sex: Difference and dominance* (1975) and Dale Spender's *Man Made*

95

Language (1980) – shifted the focus away from women as somehow deficient users of language towards men as dominating and controlling both interactions with women and the language system itself. From these books, in both cases covering a wide range of different types of research, came ideas about such areas as topic control, interruptions and verbosity, where at least research used data from real speakers rather than intuitions about idealised male and female figures.

In the process, some features of language that had been suggested previously by Robin Lakoff as markers of female uncertainty were read in very different ways when looked at in the context of a real, mixed-sex interaction. For example, Lakoff claimed that women tend to use more question forms than men, making them seem less assertive than if they had used more outright statements. In Pamela Fishman's (1977) research, women did use more question forms than men, but this was because, in the mixed-sex conversations she studied, they were frequently responsible for what is often termed 'small talk' – getting people (their male partners in this case) to open up and chat to them. Asking questions is then seen not as some universal feature of 'women's language', signalling uncertainty and powerlessness, but as part of the conversational labour women are often required to perform in their social role. This later research then had a more subtle reading of how men and women behave as a result of the roles they feel are their responsibility in interactions. This was making an important link between the features of language and their functions – the uses they are put to.

With responsibility come rights, and these two publications said much about how the linguistic rights of talk, topic control and turn-taking appeared to be distributed. For example, Zimmerman and West concluded, after studying 30 single-sex and mixed-sex conversations, that 'females are a class of speakers whose rights to speak appear to be casually infringed on by males' (1975, p. 125). This was because, in the 11 mixed-sex conversations they studied, there were 48 interruptions, 98 per cent of these by men. They saw interruption as one of several ways male speakers used to get turns and establish the topics they wanted to talk about. The researchers concluded that 'males assert an asymmetrical right to control topics' (p. 125).

While studies such as the above focused on some of the strategies used in interactions, others looked at ways of assessing talk quantitatively in order to explore the stereotype of women as the talkative sex. For example, Swacker (1975) asked men and women to talk into a tape recorder and describe a set of pictures they were given. The male speakers spoke for three times longer than the females. In the meantime, commentators such as Dale Spender were offering explanations of the seeming mismatch between the supposed talkativeness of women in the popular imagination, and their relative silence in experimental situations: that, while in research women were being measured against men, in 'folk-linguistics' they are measured against silence, which is men's preferred state for women.

From dominance to difference

The kind of work done above was useful in looking at real speakers, and in looking at how discourse strategies such as interruptions can be used to gain control of interactions. In addition, Dale Spender's focus on our written archives of language, such as dictionaries and grammar books, revealed the extent to which language is a socially constructed system rather than some natural phenomenon, and therefore can be used by powerful groups to encode their own meanings. She showed that in some respects language is 'man made' in the sex-specific as well as generic sense.

However, there was still a level of generalisation in explanations that didn't fit with many people's experience of men and women. For example, a picture seemed to emerge of bullying men and meek, oppressed women in interactions and, when the language system itself was discussed, of men sitting round conspiring how to do women out of their linguistic inheritance. Also, there was still limited exploration of context and of informants' understanding of tasks in experimental settings. For example, in the verbosity experiment mentioned above, is it that men just always talk more than women, or might there be something in the test situation that influences men and women to behave in a certain way? If a researcher came into your study group and asked the male and female students to describe a set of pictures and record themselves on tape, would you consider the results to be an accurate reflection of how much your male and female classmates normally talk?

One of the biggest difficulties, though, was that cultural differences were still not being accounted for in having categories labelled just 'men' and 'women'. For example, in what Deborah Tannen calls 'high engage-ment' cultures, where speakers have a combative style as part of their cultural rules of interaction (she quotes her own Jewish culture as one example of this), interrupting and overlapping others' speech are common features of both male and female speech. So how could variations such as these be accommodated?

Tannen's work became commercially very successful with the publication of a book in 1991 called *You Just Don't Understand: Men and women in conversation*, which was mentioned at the beginning of this unit. This book conceived the idea of difference between men and women as cultural: in other words, it asks you to suppose that men and women come from different cultures in the sense that they grow up to have completely different ideas about themselves, about their expectations, about their place in the world and about, therefore, what conversations are for. Men and women learn the rules for their own sex and then, when they interact with the opposite sex, cultural clashes can occur in the same way as they can when two speakers use different languages.

Tannen claims that there are two fundamental forces at work in social interactions: power and solidarity. We ask ourselves how much power we have in relation to the other person, and we also ask how close we are to them – how much solidarity or 'likemindedness' we have. In Tannen's view, men and women are trained to pay more attention to one or other of these dimensions, men monitoring their interactions for aspects of power, and women monitoring theirs for signals of solidarity or intimacy. We think that the rules for our own sex work across the sex divide, but they don't. So, as a result, we use the same language but we are reading the same interaction in different ways.

This approach entails a reinterpretation of many of those same aspects that were the focus for previous research. For example, if men are trained to be competitive and one such strategy is that of interruption, while women's socialisation has taught them that their role is to draw others out and establish rapport, then in mixed-sex conversations men's and women's **gender scripts** – the rules they would use for their own sex – are potentially in conflict, with resulting inequality. The difference with this interpretation is that it doesn't construct men as intentional bullies nor women as feeble victims. And our gender scripts can be analysed, understood, played with, changed and resisted.

One of the strong points of Tannen's approach is that it focuses on the thinking behind our linguistic behaviour, seeing our language use as a result of what we think we're doing when we have a conversation. In this respect, it owes much to Speech Act Theory, which saw language as performance – for example, asking, promising, apologising and so on. But Tannen's view is that the sexes may understand these various linguistic performances in different ways. For example, what do we think we are supposed to do when someone presents us with a problem – solve it or talk about it? Do we see conversation as exchanging information or as relating to the other person in some other way? How do we report back on an event – by giving the bare bones of the story, or by working it up into a fictionalised narrative, replete with juicy details? In which contexts do we feel able to talk a lot, and in which do we feel 'out of place' doing so? When we say 'sorry' are we expressing sympathy or confessing culpability? When we use reinforcements (saying 'yeah' or 'mm' when someone is speaking) do they mean 'I'm listening' or 'I agree with you'?

After difference

A shift in emphasis from 'dominance' to 'difference' has been liberating in some ways. For example, researchers have felt justified in looking at women's styles of language without starting from the view that they were either deficient or oppressed. This has meant that women could be thought of as successful language users who have their own ways to be powerful. At the same time, the idea of men being a simple locus of blame has been dissipated.

However, there have been major criticisms of 'difference' theorists, not the least of which is that they overlook the larger socio-political context. So, for example, while it might be laudable to maintain that women are very skilled at particular types of talk and that they have their own ways of 'doing gender', this means very little if we don't pay attention to how talk is valued within the wider culture. So who speaks from the pulpit, from the benches of the law courts, within the institutions of government and from our newspapers? Who are the figures who give us learned opinion on science, industry, technology and finance? Which figures are dished up again and again on literary booklists and art catalogues? Who constructs the male and female 'voices' in advertising texts? How are male and female musicians – people who really do have a 'voice' – seen and talked about? In other words, as well as looking at gender in daily interactions, we should also have a bigger vision that examines what has been called 'women's silence' in the larger culture, which often means either invisibility, or marginalisation. If this doesn't happen, then work such as Tannen's becomes, as Cameron (1995) would claim, just another advice book for women on how to talk to your man. In this sense, it would fall into line with the extract from *The Woman's Book: Contains everything a woman ought to know* (Jack and Strauss, 1911), quoted on page 82.

Another, related, criticism of 'difference' theorists is that the sexes are in important ways very *unlike* different cultures. Although we may learn what are appropriate behaviours for our own sex, we also have ideas from very early on about the opposite sex. It's a bit like saying that, if we start life with a regional accent, we don't know about Standard English until we are fully grown.

Finally, a more contemporary view of gender sees variety within this dimension rather than as a single, solid identity. Gender does not exist in isolation from factors such as ethnic origin, social class, sexuality or age, and the same 'gender' template is likely to fit across these variations only with some fairly drastic distortions. So, rather than a notion of 'femininity' or 'masculinity', we should be thinking in the plural – of femininities and masculinities. A pluralist framework also allows us to think about individual men and women adopting different identities in different contexts, according to the demands and constraints of their situation.

So does difference really exist?

In *The Myth of Mars and Venus*, Deborah Cameron points out that:

> for many linguistic variables, there is at least as much variation within each gender group as there is between the two. Focusing on the differences between groups while ignoring the differences within them is extremely misleading – but unfortunately, all too common.
>
> (2007, p. 44)

In carrying out research on gender and speech styles, and in viewing the findings of others, Cameron urges us to examine the extent to which we project on to data the very things we find there, as a result of knowing the sex of the speakers and expecting to see differences.

Activity

Read the transcripts in Text 5:3, which represent conversations that took place between colleagues at work during a coffee break.

What sex might the speakers be, in each case? Do the participants use strategies that you think are more typical of male or female speakers?

There is a commentary on this activity at the end of the unit.

Text 5:3 Coffee break conversations

Conversation 1

Speaker 1   ok?

Speaker 2   yeah (.) just feeling a bit a bit (.) sort of low (.) you know

Speaker 1   oh no (.) what's up?

Speaker 2   oh (.) just (.) rotten day and (.) well (.) sort of a a bad weekend
              really [laughs] bloody awful

Speaker 1   why (.) what happened?

Speaker 2   just usual rubbish (.) you know (.) em (.) sort of
              hassle (.) you can (.) kind of do without it and it just makes you
              feel (.) awful (.) and then (.) then you've gotta come to work

Speaker 1   hum (.) I know (.) it's just not what you need

Speaker 2   no

Conversation 2

Both colleagues have just come out of a meeting.

Speaker A   That was absolutely ridiculous

Speaker B   why?

Speaker A   WHY? (.) I've never seen anything like it (.) absolutely incredible
              (.) I don't know who the hell she thinks she is (.) but that (.) I can't
              believe she was speaking to people like that

Speaker B   I don't know (.) em (.) I thought she had a point about

Speaker A   WHAT (.) you are
              joking (.) I tell you what (.) if she ever ever spoke to me like that
              there'd be hell to pay

Speaker B   yeah but

Speaker A   and she had the nerve to say it was all our fault

Speaker B   you should (.) you should (.) tell her (.) tell

Speaker A   oh I will

Transcription key:
Underlining indicates simultaneous speech.
Square brackets contain contextual information.
Capitalisation indicates increased volume.
(.) indicates a normal pause.

Recent **meta-analysis** work – where researchers review a large number of studies on a particular topic – actually shows very little overall difference between men and women on the following aspects of linguistic behaviour (from Hyde, 2005):

vocabulary
conversational interruption
talkativeness
assertive speech
affiliative (i.e. relational) speech
self-disclosure.

The fact that there is little difference overall in these dimensions results from equivalent numbers of studies showing men and women as higher- or lower-scoring: so, for example, in some research women were seen as interrupting more, while in other studies men interrupted more. Such a contrary picture tells us something: that there is no single gender script that remains constant, where men or women talk and interact a certain way just because they are men or women. It tells us that the position or situation male and female speakers are in is the crucial factor – not just the most immediate situational factors, such as who the audience is and what the purpose of the interaction is, but also larger social factors, such as the need a speaker might feel to project a certain kind of identity.

Activity

Read the article in Text 5:4, from the US-based newspaper, the *International Herald Tribune*. Then answer the following questions:

* What does Mark Liberman mean by 'equal-opportunity prejudice'?
* What point is Janet Hyde trying to make when she says that 'Men are from North Dakota and women are from South Dakota'?
* What did Helen Thompson Woolley mean when she said in 1924 that 'scientific evidence plays very little part in producing convictions'?

Note that there is no commentary on this activity.

Text 5:4 *International Herald Tribune*

MEANWHILE ■ Ellen Goodman

The mythical chat gap

FIRST, let me clear up one small fact: Matthias Mehl is married. This will come as a shock to some of the men who e-mailed the psychologist after reading his research showing that men and women are equally talkative.

These men dismissed his work with a wave of the ring-bearing hand. "Clearly, you aren't married," they wrote. "I'm married, and let me tell you that women do talk more."

Pity poor Mehl. By disproving the notion that women were the Chatty Cathys of the species, the University of Arizona researcher had thrown science up against stereotypes. He'd put mere math up against myth.

This story began as an attempt to put a number on the chat gap between men and women. One pop psychologist after another claimed a gap of immense proportions. They said that women used 20,000 words per day to men's 7,000. Or 7,000 words a day to men's 2,000. And James Dobson, the family values guru, even claimed that God gave women 50,000 words a day and gave men a mere 25,000.

If tongues were not tied, they were hard-wired by gender. If men were from Mars and women from Venus, Mars was a taciturn planet and Venus was positively garrulous.

But Mehl decided to actually count. For the first time, some 400 college students were equipped with recording devices. It turned out, both men and women use roughly 16,000 words a day. By contrast, the range among individuals was huge. The Chattiest Carl used 47,000 words and the Silentest Sam used 700.

This got the media attention allotted to a myth-busting, man-bites-dog story on a slow news day. News? Did I say news? Mehl may have been the first who actually counted, but he was by no means the first to challenge the chat gap.

Indeed, a survey of 70 prior studies of men, women, and chatter is about to be published by University of California at Santa Cruz psychologist Campbell Leaper. This survey also shows no consistent gap in talkativeness.

Now let's acknowledge that there is a difference between the quantity and quality of words. Leaper notes that in some of the studies he reviewed, men were more likely to talk among strangers than were women, and mothers more likely to talk with their children than were fathers. If the subject was impersonal or problem-solving, men took up more of the airwaves. If it was personal, women did.

But in every situation, our similarities are far greater than the differences. So I've been wondering, when did you last hear a cry of "Vive la similarité"?

Researchers have been debunking the notion that men and women are the extremely opposite sexes since Helen Thompson Woolley first reviewed the gender research. That was in 1914. Even then, Woolley said despairingly, "the scientific evidence plays very little part in producing convictions."

Almost a century later, men's and women's lives are more alike than ever before. But we seem to have embraced old stereotypes as the new, new thing. The tale is in the book titles: "Why Men Don't Listen and Women Can't Read Maps." "Men Are Clams, Women Are Crowbars." "Why Men Don't Iron." And, of course, "Sperm Are From Men, Eggs Are From Women."

The chat gap is particularly tenacious because it's what University of Pennsylvania phonetician Mark Liberman calls "an equal-opportunity prejudice." On the one hand, be says,

When did you last hear a cry of "Vive la similarité"?

"There are people with negative attitudes toward women who see it as showing women are empty-headed chatterboxes and men are serious." But he adds, "There's another group who sees women as socially oriented, verbally adept makers of connections and men as tool-oriented, cold-hearted, unconnected loners."

When did you last hear a cry of "Vive la similarité"?

Whichever you pick, the equal-opportunity prejudice is a bulwark against change. In public life, it's easy to tag any woman who speaks up as speaking too much. In private life, wives are supposed to accept the taciturn as masculine. "Men can go home and not talk to their wives," says Leaper. "It's teaching wives to accept that he's a cave man at heart."

So here we go, once more into this breach, bearing numbers. They support the much less marketable truth about men and women that psychologist Janet Hyde whimsically describes this way: "Men are from North Dakota and women are from South Dakota."

I have no idea how long the math will trump the myth. But for now, Mehl has given us something to talk about. At around 16,000 words per day per man – and per woman. Now, is anybody out there studying how much we listen?

Ellen Goodman's column appears regularly in *The Boston Globe*.

As you have just experienced, questions about language use are complex and take some time and effort to tease out. It's much easier not to stop and think, but just roll along with the 'difference' machine as it churns out its 'research findings' in the popular Press.

Activity

Read the newspaper extract in Text 5:5, from the *Metro*, a UK freesheet.

- How convincing are the findings from this research?
- How are men and women depicted in this article?

Text 5:5 *Metro*

The women who admit: *We just can't figure out sums*

Women are nearly twice as likely as men to struggle with mental arithmetic, according to a survey.

One in three women – 34 per cent – said she has trouble adding up prices in her head while out shopping. More than half said they struggled to answer maths questions posed by their children.

But only 18 per cent of men admitted to having problems with numbers.

Overall, more than a quarter of adults reported difficulties in the survey for accountancy firm KPMG.

Older generations were more confident in their abilities than those aged between 25 and 34.

The KPMG Foundation, through its charity Every Child a Chance, is backing a Government drive to improve numeracy skills in primary schools. Charity chairman John Griffith-Jones said poor maths among adults was 'one of the greatest scourges' facing the country and it was essential that the business community became involved in tackling the problem.

Nearly half the 2,000 adults questioned said they wished they had learned more maths at school.

(Metro, January 2008)

Commentary

Although this article is not about language and communication, it still tells a story about what men and women are like, and how they supposedly differ. The article reports on research done by an accountancy firm, who of course would have a vested interest in showing that members of the public need training in the skills they can offer (at a price). Women, it seems, can't do maths. Or is it that they say they can't? Actually there is a world of difference between not being very good at something, and thinking that you're not very good at something. In this write-up of self-reported usage, women say they can't do certain kinds of adding up, while men don't report the same difficulties. Nowhere, despite the headline, is there proof of either sex's actual skill.

In the process of self-reportage, it is unclear exactly what questions were asked of participants, except for one particular question where, it seems, women were asked whether they could add up the cost of their shopping in their heads. It's unclear whether men were asked the same question, but it seems unlikely – if they had been, there might have been some reporting of the equivalent result.

This piece of press reportage of research bears the hallmarks of many accounts of male–female 'difference'. The definitive finding in the headline is somewhat at odds with the shaky 'proof' that emerges in the article; and, while it is unclear how the research was conducted, it seems that female respondents might have been asked a question that presumed gendered characteristics in the first place – women as shoppers, as housewives. But because this article taps into a whole fabric of expectations about gender and aspects of knowledge – women are not very good at scientific subjects, they are a bit scatterbrained around money (while also being rather good at spending it) – it can pass us by without critique. News articles like this provide a foundation on which stories or myths about gender are maintained on a daily basis.

Summary

This unit has explored some of society's embedded beliefs about the way men and women talk. Starting with everyday ideas encoded in popular sayings, the unit moved on to look at how the academic world has approached this topic in changing ways over the years. More recent work has questioned the whole 'difference' project on which many studies, academic and otherwise, are based. Even if differences are found, the question remains as to whether any difference is the result of speakers' maleness or femaleness, or the fact that they are in certain positions and contexts within the culture being studied. The unit ended by considering the relationship between academic research, and media reportage of difference, asking to what extent media representations maintain popular stereotypes.

Extension activities

1   Research how some of the expressions that you studied at the start of this unit are understood, by constructing a questionnaire and interviewing a range of informants.

2   In one of the extracts from Jesperson, he used the term 'instinctive' when discussing women's attitude to swearing:

> There can be no doubt that women exercise a great and universal influence on linguistic development through their instinctive shrinking from coarse and gross expressions and their preference for refined, and (in certain spheres) veiled and indirect expressions.

This gives the impression that women somehow have a 'natural' disposition to dislike 'coarse and gross expressions'. The same idea is at work in the assumption by some men in contemporary culture that they need to apologise to women for swearing in their company: 'not in front of the ladies', 'pardon my French'.

Because female reactions to swearing are often written up as something to do with women's 'natural sensitivity', there is less examination of swear words from a semantic point of view. But, if swear words are examined for their content as well as their function, we may have a different reading of women's reactions.

Read the article on 'the big C' (Text 5:6). How far do you agree with the ideas put forward here about the way men and women relate to 'the big C'?

Text 5:6 'The Big C'

Joan Smith asks why all the fuss over one little four-letter word

The big C

WHEN the writers of the Channel 4 series Mosley wanted to shock viewers in the final episode, they knew exactly what to do. They wrote a scene in which a prison guard, screaming at the jailed fascist leader, uses "the most reviled single utterance in the English language", according to scriptwriter Laurence Marks. In other words, the character calls him a vagina.

Funny business, this. The f-word has become so commonplace that it is now written not in full, without dashes or asterisks, in newspapers like the Guardian. This is not true of the other four-letter word, "an anatomical reference which will prove deeply offensive to women in particular", as the Mail on Sunday described it at the weekend, displaying a rare blend of coyness and political correctness.

You may, especially if you are a woman, feel uncomfortable about this blatant misogyny, which allows men to appropriate are important part of our anatomy and turn it into a vile insult – "a nasty name for a nasty thing" as a dictionary published in 1811 characterised it. But there is no doubt that the word has great

force. "We did it because it is immensely powerful," Marks admits. Channel 4 has defended its use in an "adult programme", screened after the 9pm watershed, but the very fact that it is being discussed before the programme has been shown, demonstrates that the decision to broadcast it is controversial.

Things were not always thus. The OED's earliest example of the word's use dates from around 1230, when the residents of Gropecunt-lane in London did not, apparently, lose sleep over the unusual name of the street where they lived. (They may have passed some happy hours in conjecture of its origin, but that is another matter.) In the 14th century, is was the standard word for the vagina; Chaucer employs it matter of factly in The Canterbury Tales, though he preferred an alternative spelling, "queynte". By Shakespeare's day, it was no longer used in polite company, although the dramatist inserted a sly pun in Hamlet, assuming his audience would pick up the reference to "country matters". In the 18th century, its use in print actually became illegal, the first conviction taking place in 1717.

So when did it acquire its power as the worst possible thing – much worse than "prick" – one human being can say to another? More to the point, why did it become so offensive? It is impossible not to make a link, as lexicographers and feminist writers have done, between the word's decline into obscenity and illegality, and fearful attitudes towards women and their sexuality.

An article in the Village Voice in New York in 1977 made this

point vividly, arguing that using the word about a man "is to call him a woman: castrated". Early attempts in the 20th century to restore its anatomical meaning, notably by DH Lawrence and James Joyce, were problematic. Mellors, in Lady Chatterley's Lover, uses it as a term of endearment, but it is hard to imagine many women enjoying the experience of being crudely equated with their sexual organs.

THIS is not to say that women haven't been tying to reclaim the word – not an easy task when men continue to cherish its status as invective. They certainly don't like to hear it from a woman and a theater group that called itself Cunning Stunts (try saying it quickly) caused consternation among male critics who feared, correctly, that something rather subversive was going on. So does its use on TV, assuming Channel 4 does not lose its nerve before Thursday, signify that the word has started on the long road, already travelled by fuck, towards frequent use, if not acceptability?

My guess is that there is a gender divide here, with some women eager to reappropriate it in protest against its anachronistic slur on female sexuality; some of my female friends use it quite deliberately when they talk about their own bodies. This is a far more effective way of removing its sting than flinging it about on Channel 4 and it makes me wonder what the lads will do if we succeed in taking away their worst insult. Perhaps it's time to start talking, pace Freud, about the terrible problems men have in overcoming their cunt envy?

Source: *The Guardian*, Tuesday March 3 1998

107

3   Research some of the different approaches taken in written academic material to male and female speech styles. Choose a particular type of material: for example, study packs aimed at primary or secondary school pupils; textbooks or academic journals aimed at older students. Try to decide which of the approaches outlined in this unit is being taken by the writer.

4   Research the way male and female speech styles are depicted in literary texts or in the popular media. Think about how you might make a comparative study: for example, a male compared with a female 'sleuth' in detective fiction; male and female characters in children's readers, comics or photostory features in magazines.

5   Conduct some interviews with male and female students in your study group (or another group of your choice, such as younger school-children) about their talk patterns. For example, when do they feel confident in talking and when not? Are there certain contexts for talk that appear to be more male- or female-dominated?

6   There have been varying accounts of male and female speech in terms of accent, particularly on how far the sexes approximate to prestige forms (for example, in the use of RP). Read the chapter entitled 'Language and sex' in Trudgill's *Sociolinguistics* (1980), which claims that women's accents are often closer to RP than those of men of the same class. Then read a critique of this approach in Spender (1980, pp. 36–8). Finally, read Milroy's *Language and social networks* (1987), which has very different findings and a different explanation of gender and accent variation. A review of all of these readings can be found in chapters 2 and 3 of Coates and Cameron (1988).

7   Research some language use on the internet, for example in msn chat. How do participants name themselves in these contexts? Are identities there freer of gender, or not, in your opinion?

Commentaries/Answers to activities

COMMENTARY: ACTIVITY p. 100, TEXT 5:3

The speakers in the transcripts are the same two men in each case, in conversations that occurred four days apart. It is possible that the speakers in Conversation 1 were seen as female, as they are engaging in talk about their feelings, with Speaker 1 drawing Speaker 2 out to express their problem, then offering sympathy and understanding. On the other hand, Conversation 2 fits a certain stereotype of male speech, containing disagreement and contradiction, and with Speaker A's raised volume and sensitivity to status issues.

In fact, what these transcripts show is that there is no single 'gender script', and that language varies quite powerfully according to context. Perhaps, though, we don't 'see' a full range of styles, but only those distinctive and narrow dimensions of difference that fit our existing stories about what men and women are like.

Discourses, identities and ideologies

Aims of this unit

In the previous units we have considered many ways in which language and other representational practices serve to construct and influence the ways in which we think about gender. But a question might have occurred to you: if gender isn't fixed and we could construct it differently, why don't we? In order to explore this question, we need to look a bit more closely at discourses and the ways in which they influence us. So in this unit the relationships between discourses, identities and ideologies, concepts introduced in the earlier units, are considered in more depth.

What is a discourse?

Discourses are difficult to define precisely, but Vivian Burr's definition of a discourse is a useful starting point. She says that a discourse is 'a set of meanings, metaphors, representations, images, stories, statements and so on that in some way together produce a particular version' of people, events or objects (1995, p. 48). Discourses provide ways of describing and framing cultural objects or categories that construct or influence how we understand them. There are many discourses available, each of which frames an object within a system of related references and associated understandings.

111

To exemplify the abstract ideas above, consider the example of foxhunting used by Vivian Burr. We can see that there are different discourses available to represent or construct hunting, via the different language choices, metaphors and images that we could use to talk about it. So hunting could be described as any of the following:

pest control
sport
animal abuse
animal cruelty
food provision.

Within each of these discourses we would expect different images and language choices to be selected to represent hunting. For example, we would not expect a pest-control discourse to include images or language that constructs animals as 'victims' or 'fluffy babies'; more likely, the language choices would refer to 'vermin' and 'damage'.

But, while some hunting discourses are mutually exclusive (such as animal abuse and sport), some can be associated and support each other. Pest control, food provision and sport are often mutually supporting hunting discourses, which in the US are also often linked to pro-gun discourses and the right to bear arms. But even in the US there are different pro-hunting sport discourses, with some believing that guns should be used while others believe in using bows and arrows.

Activity

Make a list of the sorts of images, language choices and narratives you would select for a pro-hunting pamphlet or poster and an anti-hunting pamphlet or poster. The issue should be less about what you personally believe is right or wrong, and more about how your choices create a particular story about hunting.

Note that there is no commentary on this activity.

Activity

The list below shows different descriptions or language choices that can be used to describe the same object, idea or event. What ideas and emotions are invoked or 'put into play' by these different language choices? Who is likely to use which language choices and for what reasons? What images and symbols might be associated with these choices?

    soldier – terrorist
    guerrilla – freedom fighter
    environmental activist – tree hugger
    collateral damage – deaths
    demonstrators – rioters
    murder – execution
    domestic manager – housewife
    pet owner – animal companion
    athlete – jock
    vertical dwelling – high-rise
    celebrity photographers – paparazzi
    confident – arrogant
    demonstration – civil disobedience
    dancer – stripper
    rehabilitation – detention

Note that there is no commentary on this activity.

Everyday talk is motivated

All talk is designed and **motivated**, even if we are not intentionally thinking about it. This can be difficult to accept. Language use is motivated by our understandings of the social world and how we think we fit within it. This means that the discourses that influence us are embedded in the ways we do things; that is, the ways in which we talk, draw, sing, play and so on. But we are also motivated to present ourselves and our versions as convincing, which means that we need to convince ourselves and others of the rightness of our thoughts and perceptions. We therefore invest a lot in building up particular views of the world.

We are often described as being *subject to* discourses. This phrase is used to convey the extent to which it is hard to think outside the discourse, because discourses influence the ways in which we perceive the world and this includes our sense of self – our identities. Consequently, we are emotionally invested in the discourses from which our identities arise. This is why it can be so difficult to resist established discourses and fully embrace new ideas, because it can challenge some ingrained ways of thinking about ourselves.

Activity

The 'gendered' clocks shown in Text 6:1 are similar to some of the texts you looked at in Unit two. But, rather than simply considering what gender ideas are being enacted in the clocks, consider why they are all gendered in the first place.

Text 6:1 Children's clocks

A. **Football Clock** Quartz movement; AA battery not included. 13" Diameter. #05051313 $68.00.

B. **Large Field of Dreams Clock** Baseball inset for the second hand; quartz movement. AA batteries not included. 18" Diameter. #05050138 $100.00.

C. **"All American Boy" Clock** Made from 2" x 4" wood pieces and hand painted words. AA battery not included. 14" Diameter. #05051002 $42.00.

D. **Pirate Clock** Moving pirate flag pendulum. Quartz movement; AA battery not included. 13" Diameter. #05050113 $68.00.

E. **Rascal League Clock** Moving Touchdown flag pendulum. Quartz movement; AA battery not included. 13" Diameter. #05056075 $68.00.

F. **Wild West Clock** Sheriff badge pendulum. Quartz movement; AA battery not included. 13" Diameter. #05051501 $68.00.

G. **Tea Party Clock** Charming vintage clock, complete with moving teapot pendulum. Quartz movement; AA battery not included. 13" Diameter. #05051598 $68.00.

H. **Moonlight Fairy Clock** Wooden face with decoupage, metal hands and a plastic housing for quartz movement. 10½" Diameter. #05050129 $38.00.

J. **"I Love You to the Moon" Clock** Made from 2" x 4" wood pieces and hand painted with funky glitter letters. AA battery not included. 14" Diameter. #05050304 $42.00.

K. **Little Princess Clock** Decorative pendulum. Quartz movement; AA battery not included. 13" Diameter. #05050117 $68.00.

There is no objective reason why so many inanimate gender-neutral objects are designed to be gender-specific. Of course we may prefer an object that is colourful and patterned, but the prolific use of gender-specific illustrations and the choice of pink or blue as the only options seem a little bemusing. (In Text 6:1, clock C is blue, clock J is pink, and the written descriptions for these two 'plain' clocks reveal other gendered choices.) Seeing displays of basketballs offered in pink or blue begs the question: why not red, yellow, green or purple? The preponderance of items **dichotomised** into male or female items, for example by simple (but unnecessary) colour coding, reveals the importance of gender **demarcation**. It shows us that separating the genders and denoting them as distinct is ideologically relevant, since the function is entirely social. But it also shows how gender provides a fundamental lens or explanatory framework through which we consistently see the world.

Invisible discourses, powerful practices

Discourses are powerful because we tend not to be aware of them and their influence because they become a 'natural' part of the social world and the way things are done (like having clocks that are either for a boy or girl, rather than both). Ideas about what is beautiful – or beauty discourses – are a good example of this. Most of us know and accept that the images of men and women we see in films, on television and in magazines are not typical of most men and women. We understand that female models are not typical members of the female population – that they are exceptionally tall and thin. We also know that the images in the media are often manipulated to make the women appear even more beautiful and slim and the men more muscular and well defined.

But knowing these things does not always make us feel okay about our own weight and size. In fact many researchers argue that consistently seeing so many images of these narrow versions of beauty makes us feel bad, turning the body into a project that should be improved and made beautiful. The pervasiveness of these discourses is reflected in the many television shows and other media that prominently feature 'makeovers' and other physical transformations (such as plastic surgery and dieting).

Activity

Look at the advertisement in Text 6:2 for a line of young girls' clothing. What version of femininity is represented in the ways the girls are dressed and posed? What discourses of beauty and femininity are being produced and maintained by the text?

Text 6:2 House of Deréon

Commentary

The girls in the advertisement are being used to portray glamorous, sexually desirable and attractive femininities. We are used to seeing older girls portrayed in these ways, but it feels rather shocking to see such young girls this way and raises a number of questions about the increasing social pressures on young girls. If these become the dominant discourses available from which to learn about ourselves and our value, what are the likely consequences? Some of these issues were raised in the debate about a large UK retail store selling a 'push-up' bra for 7–8-year-old girls. Some news media and online forums discussed the marketing of the bra to young girls, and part of the debate is available at www.sciforums.com/showthread.php?t=79859.

Activity

Look at the advertisement in Text 6:3. Just as the caption invites you, try and guess what product this advertisement is promoting. What are the primary ideas being sold in the advertisement?

Text 6:3 Guess what?

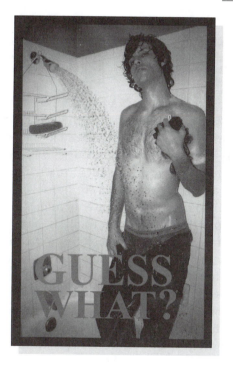

117

Commentary

The image in the advertisement mimics the increasingly adopted strategy of using sexualised imagery to sell products. This advertisement could be for shower gel, jeans, underwear or shampoo. But it is not actually selling a product. Taking a **culture jamming** approach, it was designed as a satirical parody of the increasing **commodification** of sexualised bodies. More advertisements are being designed that feature highly sexualised images of young men and women that do not even feature the product; for example, advertisements for clothing brands that feature virtually naked people – meaning the clothes being sold are not even shown. And, while we have a history of representing women in objectified and sexualised ways, there has been an increase in men being subject to these representational practices.

The increasing use of sexualised images in the media has led to many concerns about the impact of these discourses and the change in emphases and application of the common concept that 'sex sells'. Kilbourne (2005) summed up this subtle shift as a move from sex and violence promoting products to products promoting sex and violence.

One of the underlying explanations for why media images are increasingly sexual is the idea that pornographic discourses, and therefore the representational practices from those discourses, have entered mainstream discourses.

So what's the problem?

We get used to the ways that things are represented – it becomes 'natural' – and the media are a big influence in the cycle that constructs and maintains discourses. But it also becomes natural for us to think of ourselves and the world within the discourses with which we are most familiar, to the extent that we do not question what we are being shown, what is available and how we should see ourselves. So, even if we do become aware of discourses and the powerful influence that language and representational practices have over us, it is hard for us not to be influenced by them. Like the beauty discourses, even if we know it's not real, and we know that 'looks aren't important', it is hard not to want to have 'fab abs' – whether you're a boy or a girl.

This happens because our identities are embedded in discourses, and the discourses that we learn are those that dominate our worlds, that provide and describe our experiences. As you discovered in Unit two, we learn what we are from the social world. This means that the increased sexualisation of both genders will be influencing who we think we are and how we should think about ourselves. But we don't get to hear and see all discourses equally.

Activity

Look at the options available in the selection of dolls 'just like me' in Text 6:4. What physical characteristics are available and what does this tell us about the category 'girls'?

Text 6:4 Just like me?

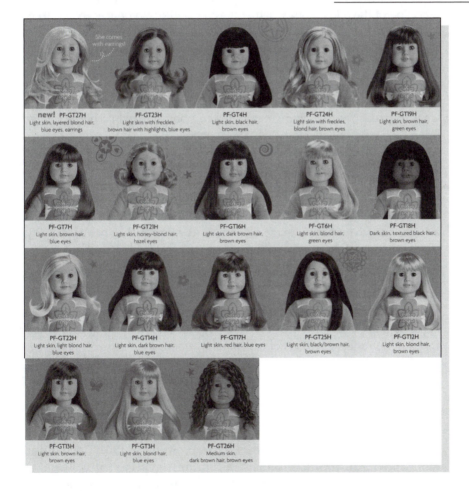

Commentary

The 'like me' doll types have a wide range of whiteness represented, with limited options for other ethnic groups. For example, all the dolls have long straight, straight 'textured', or slightly wavy hair. Such practices represent the **privileged** positioning of whiteness in Western cultures, to the extent that whiteness is often not even considered an ethnicity. Whiteness is the natural state – or unmarked form – against which other ethnicities are marked, hence it is invisible as an ethnic form but highly visible in mainstream representational practices. This effectively constructs a limited version of girls – one that is dominated by a deep understanding and familiarity with the variation in the category of whiteness, but a limited variation of other ethnicities.

The ideas and discourses that get used in any text or situation are a reflection of the originators, whether they are authors, producers or speakers. This means that we see and hear more of the discourses of those who are in the position to be seen and heard. Sport is a good example of this, with evidence that shows a consistent bias in what is shown and how it is shown. For example, Sabo *et al.* (1996) reported on the race, ethnic and nationalistic bias of television sports coverage, while Billings *et al.* (2002) reported on the ways in which sports commentators talked about basketball players based upon their own underlying beliefs about gender.

Sport is a highly masculine discourse, meaning that we tend to think of and construct sport as a male activity and interest. In fact, sport is so masculinised that it is associated with **hypermasculinity** and heterosexuality. This means that male athletes are assumed to be heterosexual, while female athletes have to demonstrate their femininity to manage their heterosexuality, simply because of their participation in such a male domain (Caudwell, 1999).

The dominant discourses that construct gender, femininity, masculinity and sexuality are mutually supportive and literally embodied in male and female bodies. This is why male dancers and female athletes with big muscles make us think in sexually stereotypical ways, because otherwise they would threaten our understandings of the 'natural' world.

Prominence and dominance

The ideas from dominant discourses are more often talked about and represented as if they are factual – a form of privilege that is linked to **hegemony** because the discourses that become dominant are those that serve the people who are powerful. But these people are also products of the dominant discourses, meaning that their identities and understandings are subject to these discourses, making it hard for them to see any real problems with the way things are. However, those who are not in power are also subject to the same powerful discourses, meaning that they may also believe in the ideas that are dominant, even if it oppresses them (van Dijk, 1993).

This is rather complicated, but can be understood if we think back to ideas that were once considered to be fact. For example, in the UK and the US there was a widespread belief – or hegemony – that girls should not be educated; that they were incapable of learning. At the time this idea was supported by scientists, religious leaders, educators and politicians – who were all men, because women could not hold such positions. Men were the people who had power and whose power was embedded in discourses that influenced social action, such as who got to vote and who was suitable to hold political positions and make the rules. However, many women also believed they should not be educated, because they too were subject to the gender hegemony – even if it wasn't in their best interests. Fortunately, enough women and men resisted this hegemony and fought to change the definitions of women and men embedded in the dominant discourses at that time.

Of course, it's easy to look back and see the problems with historical forms of dominant hegemonies, but it's much harder to see and resist the current ones. It takes some effort actively to resist and change our ingrained assumptions. In fact, Sanjay Gupta (2008) describes some research showing that actively rethinking and challenging the dominance of traditional beauty discourses using 'body activism' – a form of civil disobedience – has helped raise young people's awareness and resistance to unrealistic body images more successfully than simply 'knowing' about their effects.

Summary

This unit explored how discourses are often invisible, naturalised and hard to resist because our own identities are based upon them. But hopefully you also realised that we can resist them rather than simply accept them. Critical questioning requires effort to recognise implicit biases and practices in order to become more aware of the way we see the world, and to actively question and disrupt the way it is represented both for us and by us.

Extension activities

1   Select some particular magazines (decide if you want to look at magazines for teenagers or adults, males or females) and count the advertisements that use sexualised or non-sexualised images. Consider what they are selling and whether the product is present or not. What messages or discourses about men and women do the images and products suggest? You could extend this by comparing magazines for men and women.

2   This unit has shown particular examples of the way girls and women are represented in sexualised ways. But sexualised images of boys and men are increasingly common, particularly in advertising. Look at the advert in Text 6:5 and explain how the sexualised image of the male figure works: What kind of masculinity is being sold?; Who are the 'ladies' who are being addressed (and who is addressing them?); What intertextual messages are being referred to?

Text 6:5 Something for the weekend

3   Select some music videos and discuss in what ways they represent men and women. What sorts of ideas and images are commonly used? Is there a difference across music genres? Is there a difference between male and female musicians?

4   Design a campaign for a widely gendered or sexualised product that either challenges gender stereotypes, uses counter-stereotypical images, and/or does not use sexualised images.

5   Analyse the sports news to see who gets reported and how they get represented. What sort of information is given about them? Are they hypermasculinised, sexualised or made comical?

further
reading

All the books in the INTERTEXT series, including the core text, cover aspects of language and gender as an integral part of each topic. *The Language of Advertising* and *The Language of Newspapers* both have a strong focus on gender in the language of mass media texts.

If you are interested in exploring further ideas about analysing texts, try S. Mills (1995) *Feminist Stylistics*, London: Routledge.

'Political correctness' as an issue can be seen within larger questions about language correctness in general in D. Cameron (1995) *Verbal Hygiene*, London: Routledge.

D. Cameron (ed.) (1998) *The Feminist Critique of Language*, London: Routledge, and S.Mills (ed.) (1995) *Language and Gender: Interdisciplinary perspectives*, Harlow: Longman both take a good interdisciplinary approach, so that questions about language and gender are related to issues of social and political power. The former text is particularly useful for its historical perspective.

If you are interested in work on how gender, identity and relationships are expressed in everyday popular texts, then look at K. Harvey and C. Shalom (eds) (1997) *Language and Desire*, London: Routledge.

An older book, but one that still has interesting things to say about gender and popular culture is R. Coward (1984) *Female Desire*, London: Paladin.

If you would like to explore further the extent to which our lives are socially constructed (as opposed to 'natural'), then read V. Burr (1995) *An Introduction to Social Constructionism*, London: Routledge.

The relationship between language and cognitive representation is explored further in S.K. Ng (2007) 'Language-based discrimination: blatant and subtle forms', *Journal of Language and Social Psychology* 26: 106–22.

An introduction to neuromarketing can be found in D.L. Fugate (2007) 'Neuromarketing: a layman's look at neuroscience and its potential application to marketing practice', *Journal of Consumer Marketing* 24: 385–94.

Finally, the following texts offer many interesting ideas on approaches to research, particularly in their treatment of variety and diversity: V. Bergwall, J. Bing and A. Freed (1996) *Rethinking Language and Gender Research*, Harlow: Longman; and K. Hall and M. Buchholtz (1995) *Gender Articulated*, London: Routledge.

In J. Coates and D. Cameron (eds) (1988) *Women in their Speech Communities*, Harlow: Longman, you can also find further discussion of work done in previous years on sex differences in language, such as ideas about gender and Standard English. This book would therefore support the work you did in Unit five.

D. Cameron (2007) *The Myth of Mars and Venus*, Oxford: Oxford University Press also supports Unit five by reviewing how research on language and speech styles has been interpreted over the years.

references

Amis, M. (1997) *Night Train*, London: Jonathan Cape.

Berger, J. (1972) *Ways of Seeing*, Harmondsworth: British Broadcasting Corporation/ Penguin.

Billings, A.C., Halone, K.K. and Denham, B.E. (2002) '"Man, that was a pretty shot": an analysis of gendered broadcast commentary surrounding the 2000 men's and women's NCAA final four basketball championships', *Mass Communication and Society* 5: 295–315.

Bodine, A. (1975) 'Andocentrism in prescriptive grammar: singular "they", sex-indefinite "he", and "he or she"', *Language in Society* 4: 129–46. Reprinted in D. Cameron (ed.) *The Feminist Critique of Language: A reader*, London: Routledge, pp. 124–38.

Burr, V. (1995) *An Introduction to Social Construction*, London and New York: Routledge.

Cameron, D. (1995) *Verbal Hygiene*, London: Routledge.

Cameron, D. (2007) *The Myth of Mars and Venus*, Oxford: Oxford University Press.

Caudwell, J. (1999) 'Women's football in the United Kingdom', *Journal of Sport and Social Issues* 23: 390–402.

Chandler, D. (1997) *Writing Oneself in Cyberspace*. Available online at www.aber.ac.uk/media/Documents/short/homepgid.html (accessed 3 June 2008).

Channell, J. (1994) *Vague Language*, Oxford: Oxford University Press.

Coates, J. and Cameron, D. (1988) *Women in their Speech Communities*, Harlow: Longman.

Coward, R. (1984) 'The sex life of stick insects', in R. Coward, *Female Desire*, London: Paladin.

Crowther, B. and Leith, D. (1995) 'Feminism, language, and the rhetoric of television wildlife programmes', in S. Mills (ed.) *Language and Gender: Interdisciplinary perspectives*, Harlow: Longman.

Daly, M. and Caputi, J. (1987) *Websters' First New Intergalactic Wickedary of the English Language*, London: The Women's Press.

Dorling Kindersley Children's Dictionary (1996) London: Dorling Kindersley. Available as CD-ROM.

Dubois, B. and Crouch, I. (1975) 'The question of tag questions in women's speech: they don't really use more of them, do they?', *Language in Society* 4: 289–94.

Elgin, S. (1981) 'Some proposed additions to the glossary of needed lexical items for the expression of women's perceptions', *Lonesome Node* 1(l). (A range of Elgin's work is discussed in R. Bailey (1991) *Images of English: A cultural history of the language*, Cambridge: Cambridge University Press.)

Elgin, S. (1985) *Native Tongue*, London: Women's Press.

Elgin, S. (1987) *Native Tongue II*, New York: DAW Books.

Ellis, H. (1904), cited in Jesperson, O. (1922) *Language: Its nature, development and origin*, New York: Allen & Unwin.

Fishman, P. (1977) 'Interactional shitwork', *Heresies: A Feminist Publication on Arts and Politics* 2: 99–101.

Gupta, S. (2008) 'Taking on the thin ideal', *Time*, 9 June, p. 50.

Harvey, K. (1997) 'Everybody loves a lover', in K. Harvey and C. Shalom (eds) *Language and Desire*, London: Routledge.

Herriman, J. (1998) 'Descriptions of *woman* and *man* in present-day English', *Moderne Språk* XCII (2): 136–42.

Hoeg, P. (1994) *Miss Smilla's Feeling for Snow*, London: Flamingo Books.

Horwood, F.C. (ed.) (1971) *A.E. Housman: Poetry and prose, a selection*, London: Hutchinson.

Hudson, J. (1999) Personal correspondence.

Hyde, J. (2005) 'The gender similarities hypothesis', *American Psychologist* 60(6): 581–92.

Jack, F.B. and Strauss, R. (1911) *The Woman's Book: Contains everything a woman ought to know*, London: T.C. and E.C. Jack.

Jesperson, O. (1922) *Language: Its nature, development and origin*, New York: Allen & Unwin.

Johnson, F.L. and Young, K. (2002) 'Gendered voices in children's television advertising', *Critical Studies in Media Communication* 19: 461–80.

Jones, M. (1999) Personal correspondence, University of Nottingham.

Kilbourne, J. (2005) 'What else does sex sell', *International Journal of Advertising* 24: 119–22.

Khosroshahi, F. (1989) 'Penguins don't care but women do: a social identity analysis of a Whorfian problem', *Language in Society* 18: 505–25.

Lakoff, G. (1987) *Women, Fire and Dangerous Things: What categories reveal about the mind*, Chicago, IL: University of Chicago Press.

Lakoff, R. (1975) *Language and Woman's Place*, New York: Harper & Row.

Lamb, C. (1980) *Seduction*, Richmond: Harlequin Mills & Boon Ltd.

Lochhead, L. (1986) *Dreaming Frankenstein*, Edinburgh: Polygon.

McConnell-Ginet, S. (1998) 'The sexual (re)production of meaning: a discourse-based theory', in D. Cameron (ed.) *The Feminist Critique of Language*, London: Routledge.

Miller, C. and Swift, K. (1981) *The Handbook of Non-Sexist Writing*, London: The Women's Press.

Milroy, L. (1987) *Language and Social Networks*, Oxford: Blackwell.

Morgan, G. (1986) *Images of Organization*, London: Sage.

Ng, S.H. (1990) 'Language and control', in H. Giles and W.P. Robinson (eds) *Handbook of Language and Social Psychology*, Chichester: John Wiley & Sons Ltd.

O'Barr, W. and Atkins, B. (1980) '"Women's language" or "powerless language"?', in S. McConnell-Ginet, N. Furman and N. Borker (eds) *Women and Language in Literature and Society*, New York: Praeger.

Paugh, A. (2005) 'Learning about work at dinnertime: language socialization in dual-earner American families', *Discourse & Society* 16(1): 55–78.

Policy Studies Institute (1989) *Cultural Trends*, London: Policy Studies Institute.

Rich, A. (1979) *On Lies, Secrets and Silence*, New York: Norton.

Sabo, D., Jansen, S.C., Tate, D., Duncan, M.C. and Leggett, S. (1996) 'Televising international sport: race, ethnicity, and nationalistic bias', *Journal of Sport & Social Issues* 20: 7–21.

Smith, D. (1978) 'A peculiar eclipsing: women's exclusion from man's culture', *Women's Studies International Quarterly* 1: 281–96.

Spender, D. (1980) *Man Made Language*, London: Pandora.

Swacker, M. (1975) 'The sex of the speaker as a sociolinguistic variable', in B. Thorne and N. Henley (eds) *Language and Sex: Difference and dominance*, Rowley, MA: Newbury House.

Tannen, D. (1991) *You Just Don't Understand: Men and women in conversation*, London: Virago.

Thorne, B. and Henley, N. (eds) (1975) *Language and Sex: Difference and dominance*, Rowley, MA: Newbury House.

Trudgill, P. (1980) *Sociolinguistics*, Harmondsworth: Penguin.

US Dept of Labor (1975) *Job Title Revisions*, 3rd edn, Washington, DC: US Dept of Labor.

van Dijk, T.A. (1993) 'Principles of critical discourse analysis', *Discourse and Society* 4: 249–83.

Whorf, B.L. (1956) 'Science and linguistics', in J.B. Carroll (ed.) *Language, Thought and Reality*, Cambridge, MA: MIT Press.

Wilson, T. (1560) *Arte of Rhetorique*, Scolars Facsimiles and Reprints, originally London: John Kingston. (Cited in Bodine, A. (1975) 'Androcentrism in prescriptive grammar: singular "they", sex-indefinite "he", and "he or she"', *Language in Society* 4: 129–46.)

Zimmerman, D. and West, C. (1975) 'Sex roles, interruptions and silences in conversation', in B. Thorne and N. Henley (eds) *Language and Sex: Difference and dominance*, Rowley, MA: Newbury House.

index of
terms

This is a form of combined glossary and index. Listed below are some of the key terms used in the book, together with brief definitions for purposes of reference. The page references will normally take you to the first use of the term in the book, where it will be shown in bold.

anthropomorphism 6
A view that an animal or an object has feelings like those of a human being. A similar term is 'personification'. From Greek *anthropos*, 'human', and *morphe*, 'form'.

antonyms 55
Words that are opposite in meaning, such as 'clean' and 'dirty'.

arbitrary 3
Random, unconnected. When applied to language, it suggests that there is no intrinsic connection between language and its **referents**.

cognition 42
A broad term that covers the area of mental events: the processes, structures and events through which we perceive, interpret and behave in the physical and social world. This includes thinking, reasoning, knowledge, memory, perception, etc.

cognitive model 46
A 'mental' concept or representation of the knowledge we have about everything – people, animals, objects, events, attitudes, emotions,

etc. This even includes our understanding of physical things such as gravity – what it is and how it works.

collocation 25
The repeated occurrence of words in the company of others, sometimes even in a set order, for example 'fish and chips', 'bed and breakfast', 'men and women'.

commodification 118
The transformation or use of an object, idea or person as a product for consumption, typically for economic gain.

connotation 22
A level of meaning that is based on the associations surrounding a word. For example, the word 'child' could suggest ideas of purity and innocence (see also **denotation**).

culture jamming 118
Difficult to define precisely, this broadly involves the satirical and ironic use of representational practices and techniques to reveal, critique and subvert dominant cultural forms; particularly those associated

with mass media, **commodification** and consumption.

deficit model 92
A model that ascribes fault or the lack of ability in the group being referred to.

demarcation 115
Defining and delineating as segregated and different.

denotation 22
The barest, dictionary definition of a word. For example, the denotation for 'child' would be 'young human being' (see also **connotation**).

deviant 54
A person, event or behaviour that does not fit the **norm** or expectations, hence the phrase 'to deviate from the norm'. Often the term 'deviant' has negative **connotations** and is typically used to refer to people or things that go beyond or fall outside socially acceptable boundaries – for example, 'a sexual deviant'.

dichotomised 115
The situation where items, experiences and beliefs are separated into two oppositional and contradictory positions.

discourse 4
A system of representation, related references and associated understandings that frame an object, event or person in a particular way. (See Unit six for an expansion of this definition.)

discrimination 4
The process of making distinctions; the process by which we distinguish between objects, events, categories, etc.

euphemism 26
A polite alternative expression for an area that is considered taboo. For example, the phrases 'sleeping with' and 'making love' are euphemisms for sexual intercourse. The opposite of a euphemism is called a 'dysphemism'. This refers to a deliberately crude alternative, such as 'shag'.

fire 42
A technical term that describes the action of nerve cells (**neurones**) when they communicate or pass a chemical signal to other nerve cells. Firing involves an electrical impulse that triggers the release of a chemical messenger (a neurotransmitter).

folklinguistics 83
Ideas about language encoded in popular sayings such as proverbs.

gender scripts 98
The idea that the sexes adopt roles that are deemed appropriate to their sex, and express these roles in broad aspects of behaviour, rather as actors who have learnt roles and lines for performance.

generic reference 58
The ability of a term to refer generally.

hegemony 120
Power, control or dominating influence over cultural, social and political spheres, including definitions and practices.

hypermasculinity 120
An accentuated form of masculinity that emphasises traditional male characteristics, such as competitiveness, aggression, strength, etc.

hyponyms 51

Members of a category. For example, 'apple' and 'pear' are hyponyms of the category 'fruit'.

identity 29

The sense we have of ourselves and others as individuals and group members, and the 'story' or version of the individual that is portrayed and perceived.

ideology 48

A system of beliefs and ideas characteristic of a society, group or individual. This system influences thinking and explanations, and determines policies and practices.

intertextuality 67

The way in which one text echoes or refers to another text. Intertextuality can operate at many different levels, from single words or phrases to whole genres of text.

marking 41

The process or act of signalling an alternative meaning to 'normal'. Signalling a specific meaning that would otherwise be missed or incorrectly understood.

meta-analysis 102

Obtaining an overview of a wide range of research studies.

metaphor 43

A word or phrase that establishes a comparison or analogy between one object or idea and another. For example, saying that a woman has been 'left on the shelf' draws a comparison between women and saleable commodities.

metonymy 12

Often seen as a type of metaphor, metonymy refers to objects or ideas by using features often associated with them. For example, saying 'suits' instead of 'businessmen' in a sentence such as 'Two suits came into the room.'

modifier 27

A word or phrase that adds more detail (or modifies) another element. For example, in the phrase 'male nurse', the adjective 'male' modifies the noun 'nurse'.

morphology 57

The different structural elements that are combined to form words. For example, in the word 'spinster' there are two morphemes, 'spin' (in the sense of cloth) and 'ster', which means 'female doer of action'. So a spinster was originally a female spinner of yarn. The morpheme 'ster' can be seen in some surnames, such as Baxter ('bakster' – female baker) and Brewster (female brewer).

motivated 113

Having a reason, incentive, interest or commitment. In this case, one is motivated to construct and maintain one's own **identities**, ideas and related **discourses**.

narratee 33

The implied reader of a text. The identity of the narratee is established by sets of assumptions in the text about what the person reading it is like. (The narrator is the person in a text who appears to be addressing the reader.)

neuromarketing 50

A new area of study that combines cognitive science and marketing to explore the relationship between consumer behaviour and brain functions and processes. The aim, ultimately, is to be able to understand and influence consumer behaviour.

neurones 42
The cells of the nervous system (including the brain and spinal cord) that communicate or transmit information around the body.

norms 51
Rules or standards shared by a group of people that are held or believed to be the most common, frequent or acceptable, and that are used to guide behaviour and make judgements, decisions, etc.

patriarchal 74
Male-controlled. The literal meaning of 'patriarch' is 'head of the family unit'. The term refers to the way in which men have traditionally been the head of the household, and the way in which property laws and naming conventions have traditionally followed the male line of inheritance.

phallocratic 74
Male-centred, and/or the idea that the male sex is superior. From the Latin *phallus*, 'penis'.

privileged 120
Being in a position to take advantage of all the resources in a society. Particularly relevant in modern times is access to the media.

pronoun reference 10
This is an aspect of cohesion, or the way in which texts are woven together, particularly across sentence boundaries. Pronoun reference is the linking together of pronouns with other linguistic items. In the following example,

the pronoun 'he' links back to the proper noun 'Bill': 'I went to work yesterday and saw *Bill*. *He* was looking very tanned.'

prototype 52
A type of cognitive model that represents the typical or ideal defining characteristics of a category.

received opinion 91
Views that are held as correct by the more powerful groups within an establishment.

received pronunciation (RP) 93
A social class accent that was officially 'received' in royal circles (hence the name), and that has traditionally been seen as prestigious.

referent 26
An object, person or idea that is being referred to.

representational practices 32
The ways in which things are put into action or the practices used when representing (picturing, discussing) ideas, people, etc.

rhetorical 66
Persuasive. Historically, the term 'rhetoric' described the study of the persuasive techniques used in speechmaking in Ancient Greece.

salient 4
Meaningful, important, relevant, pertinent or requiring (cognitive) attention.

sex-specific reference 58
The way in which a term refers specifically to one sex or the other.

The Language and Sexuality Reader

Deborah Cameron and Don Kulick

The Language and Sexuality Reader is the first of its kind to bring together material from the fields of anthropology, communication studies, linguistics, medicine and psychology in an examination of the role of sexuality in written and spoken language. The text begins by guiding students through early study in the field from the 1940s to the 1980s, where the focus is homosexual language, and its difference from the heterosexual mainstream. The second part of the Reader widens the focus: moving away from the generic labels of 'homosexual' and 'heterosexual', it explores the diversity of linguistic and sexual practices as documented and debated among scholars from the mid-1990s to the present.

Organised into thematic sections, the Reader addresses:

*   Early documentation of vocabulary used by male homosexuals; including Gershon Legman's glossary of 1941, and later work on the existence of a discourse style signifying gay identity
*   The use of language by individuals to present themselves as sexual and gendered subjects
*   The way language reflects, reinforces or challenges cultural norms defining what is 'natural' and desirable in the sphere of sex
*   The verbal communication of sexual desire in different settings, genres and media.

Contributors include: Hideko Abe, Laura Ahearn, Rusty Barrett, Deborah Cameron, Kathryn Campbell-Kibler, Donald W. Cory, Justine Coupland, Louie Crew, James Darsey, Penelope Eckert, Susan Ehrlich, Joseph J. Hayes, Scott Kiesling, Celia Kitzinger, Don Kulick, William L. Leap, Gershon Legman, Momoko Nakamura, Sally McConnell-Ginet, Julia Penelope, Robert J. Podesva, June Machover Reinisch, Sarah J. Roberts, Stephanie A. Sanders, David Sonenschein, David Valentine.

Deborah Cameron is a sociolinguist, and currently holds the Rupert Murdoch Chair of Language and Communication at Oxford University. Her previous publications include *Verbal Hygiene* (1995) and *The Feminist Critique of Language* (1998). **Don Kulick** is Professor of Anthropology and director of the Center for the Study of Gender and Sexuality at New York University. His books include *Travesti* (1998) and the co-edited *Fat*. Together, Deborah Cameron and Don Kulick are the authors of *Language and Sexuality* (2003).

ISBN13: 978-0-415-363082 (hbk)
ISBN13: 978-0-415-36307-5 (pbk)

Related titles from Routledge

Literacy and Gender

Researching texts, contexts, and readers

Gemma Moss

Part of the Literacies *series*

'In the context of continuing debates about how to teach reading, and about boys' underachievement, Gemma Moss brings us right up close to what children are actually doing with books in classrooms. Her ethnographic research is meticulous and fine-grained, and she presents some striking findings about how the dynamics between literacy, gender and attainment are configured within particular schools and classrooms. This accessible, subtle book raises important questions for current policy makers and is recommended reading for anyone who cares about children, literacy and education.' Janet Maybin, *The Open University*, UK.

Why are girls outperforming boys in literacy skills in the Western education system today? To date, there have been few attempts to answer this question. *Literacy and Gender* sets out to redress this state of affairs by re-examining the social organisation of literacy in primary schools.

In studying schooling as a social process, this book focuses on the links between literacy, gender and attainment, the role school plays in producing social difference and the changing pattern of interest in this topic both within the feminist community and beyond. Gemma Moss argues that the reason for girls' relative success in literacy lies in the structure of schooling and in particular the role the reading curriculum plays in constructing a hierarchy of learners in class. Using fine-grained ethnographic analysis of reading in context, this book outlines methods for researching literacy as a social practice and understanding how different versions of what counts as literacy can be created in the same site.

Literacy and Gender makes a valuable contribution to current debates about literacy pedagogy and outlines a principled basis upon which to review the literacy curriculum in action.

Gemma Moss is Reader in Education at the Institute of Education, University of London.

ISBN13: 978-0-415-23456-6 (hbk)
ISBN13: 978-0-415-23457-3 (pbk)

Available at all good bookshops
For ordering and further information please visit:
www.routledge.com